BLOOD SPORT

FORMULA ONE DRIVERS
OF THE DEADLY YEARS

MARY SCHNALL HEGLAR
Author, *The Grand Prix Champions*
a *Road & Track* book

outskirts
press

Outskirts Press, Inc.
http://www.outskirtspress.com

ISBN: 978-1-9772-0237-6

Outskirts Press and the "OP" logo are trademarks belonging to Outskirts Press, Inc.

Foreword

The dazzling sport of Formula One has a black and violent past. Global celebrities and fabled locations and glamour have long been part of the thrilling grand prix scene, but all the bells and whistles in the world cannot hide the bloody costs in the history of the sport I love.

Formula One suffered extreme growing pains during the late 1960s and early 1970s, when technology began to push beyond the capabilities of measures to contain it, and the risk level shot off the charts.

Of the 49 F1 drivers in this book, 10 perished in race cars, some as thousands watched, others as deep inside lonely woods as their hurtling cars could throw them. Another four were killed in violent accidents away from the track. Only 14 died of natural causes, and only nine of those reached their 70s or beyond.

Time is running out for us F1 journalists of that era to share first-hand experiences from that most lethal period in grand prix history. I knew the drivers and photographed them during those glorious, terrible years, so it's time to share my personal impressions and encounters with these legendary men. From my private collection I've added photos not published until now.

You're about to meet the drivers of those deadly years, many of whose names still resonate down all the years since their headline-making triumphs and tragedies.

Table of Contents

CHAPTER 1

Rolling The Dice

The men in this book risked their lives every time they stepped into a race car. They gambled not only their lives but their sight, their hearing, their ability to walk and move. Many of them stifled their desire for marriage and a family, not wanting to carry the burden of family worries or inflict racing worries on a loved one. All of them surrendered a "normal" life for one of constant travel, hotel rooms, forced social events, relentless pressures.

All that risk and frantic lifestyle for what? To scratch an itch. To challenge, to compete, to excel. To go faster than anyone else. To fear and then conquer. And back in the early days of F1, to survive, because they joined a sport that quite likely would kill them before long.

Why were they so willing to risk so much? To them, the answer was self-evident. The essence of all their answers was, risk simply came with the territory. For a driver, it wasn't complicated: He raced cars, and if he died doing it, so be it. Graham Hill pointed out that it's risky just going through a normal day—crossing the street, going swimming, and so on. "It's just a question of degree," he told me; "We [drivers] spend our lives trying to minimize the risk and avoiding it, more than most people. But of course we do put ourselves in the front line . . . " Stirling Moss shared a slightly different take: "I just thought that when anything happened, I had sufficient experience that I most likely could cope, and I had by experience coped with a hell of a lot of funny things happening."

By putting up with those "funny things," they enabled themselves to push limits personal and technical beyond what was thought possible, and to do what they loved doing above all else.

Today those at the top can become wealthy, but back in the day, financial rewards were few and far between. Drivers often paid their own way, racing for just a small share of any prize money, which wasn't much. In the 1960s, Stirling parlayed his reputation into a marketable product and gathered in a few sponsors. As the 1970s unrolled, savvy drivers such as Jackie Stewart envisioned what the celebrity angle could mean to a commercial business, and F1 exploded onto the scene big-time.

The photos in this book reflect the days when media people were allowed to roam the pits. Shots that only a few special media folks are privy to today were taken by the dozens back in the '60s and '70s. Some of my colleagues were professional photographers, and most of the rest of us carried cameras. I was there gathering material for what became *The Grand Prix Champions,* published by the book arm of *Road & Track*; it covers each man who earned the World Championship in the first 25 seasons, from Farina through Fittipaldi.

Inside my latest book, *Blood Sport,* are photos and some of my personal impressions of 49 drivers and five team owners/constructors from that era. In these never-published photos, you'll see Jackie Stewart as he fights the terrible strains of racing. There's Max Mosley as he struggles to stay afloat. Graham Hill epitomizing the lion in winter. Stirling Moss being . . . well, Stirling Moss. Phil Hill at home. Emmo Fittipaldi in conference with Colin Chapman. Bruce McLaren ready to go out and win another Can-Am.

With Formula One bursting back onto the American scene, it seemed time to pull these encounters and photographic gems from my files and share them with you.

CHAPTER 2

The Cutting Edge
Draws Blood

The 1960s and '70s witnessed some of F1 racing's most golden yet darkest years. The names of Clark, Stewart, McLaren, Brabham, Gurney were writ large. The glow from their exploits bathed grand prix in a magical light. Yet the shadow looming over the sport was black and growing blacker: Drivers were being killed at a shocking, relentless rate.

Men had died in their race cars since the beginning. What was suddenly happening to snuff out so many more, so regularly? Why now?

Possible answers lie in the very element that makes motor racing so thrilling: speed. Technological acceleration swooped across all areas of Formula One in the 60s and '70s. And before long, technology was outrunning the ability to control it.

Fatalities

Formula One suffered severe growing pains when cutting edge technology began drawing blood. Lighter cars flew faster around circuits that hadn't changed in decades. Tire treads had less adhesion at higher speeds. Struts and wheels and transmissions and bodywork buckled under the enormous g-forces generated under ever-increasing speeds. In one ten-year period that I call the Deadly Decade, 1965-1975, at least 17 F1 drivers were killed. In 1968 alone, one F1 driver was killed every month for four straight months. 1970 claimed four more lives.

The carnage was horrific, and all those tragedies piled up until pressure built for preventing race deaths. Obvious? Yes, to most of us and on hindsight. But there was immense resistance to inserting safety measures into F1 (just as today, with the advent of the halo). Surprisingly, most of the resistance came from the drivers themselves (just as today). One aspect of a race driver's thinking is that it's always the other fellow who gets hurt or killed. Is that a mad fantasy of complete control? Maybe, but each driver *was* in complete control back then: Each was alone in the cockpit with only an occasional pit board to connect him to his team; each was the sole source of performance information during development and testing; and each ultimately determined his own speed and strategy throughout a race. Concerning safety measures, many drivers felt that if they themselves were willing to risk their lives, what was all the fuss about?

Safety Features

Of the drivers campaigning for better safety, Jackie Stewart and Jo Bonnier led the way. Of the non-drivers, BRM owner Louis Stanley and Sid Watkins, M.D., weighed in heavily. These men and others raised the specters of *preventable* deaths, *unnecessary* obstacles, *unsafe* procedures, *lethal* lacks, *unacceptable* risks. They relentlessly promoted the use of on-board fire extinguishers, stronger cockpits, better fire suits and masks, gloves and helmets, more seat belts, improved driver communication with the pits, more capable marshals and volunteers, bigger run-off areas, slick tires, wheel tethers, better road surfaces, more flexible roadside barriers, advanced equipment and personnel in the circuit medical centers, and on and on—none of which would degrade the excitement of the race for either the drivers or the fans.

Most changes were expensive. But the cost in dollars versus the cost in human lives became an invalid controversy in the eyes of more and more racing people, and the safety group eventually won out.

In a gradual progression, grand prix racing grew safer for everyone— the drivers, the pit crews, team personnel, the media, the fans. Until the autumn of 2014 when Jules Bianchi had his fatal accident, no F1 driver had been killed in a race car since Roland Ratzenberger and Ayrton Senna in one terrible weekend in 1994.

Advances didn't occur just on the engineering side of grand prix racing; salaries and the schedule accelerated, too—with game-changing consequences.

Salaries

Instead of just a share of any prize money, a driver began to get a small salary from his team. Then he began selling his high-profile exposure to product sponsors, who paid him goodly amounts to plaster their decals on his car. Pedro Rodriguez perfectly illustrates how it worked:

For 1970, Pedro was paid $30,000 by the BRM team. For 1971, the team paid him nothing but allowed him 100% of the income on four decals/sponsor slots. He sold each decal for around $70,000 for that year. In 1992, Ayrton Senna earned $22M from salaries plus endorsements. In 2013, Lewis Hamilton and Fernando Alonso each earned $25M *in team salary alone.* In 2015, Lewis became the $50M man when he signed a $150M three-year deal. In 2017, Fernando Alonso gathered up over $300K for his drive at the Indy 500—where he DNF. Jaw-dropping amounts continue to climb, surely leaving driver-suited ghosts shaking their heads.

Schedule

Every decade reflects an increase in the number of championship F1 races. The first year of the World Driving Championship, 1950, saw six races. Nine were on the 1960 calendar. By 1970 the original number had more than doubled. For 2019, there are 21 races.

Once the grand prix schedule expanded, drivers had less time and less financial need to race outside F1. More grands prix, more risk, adding to the F1 fatality statistics that were starting to climb.

Consequences

Thanks to the often-ridiculed and unflagging efforts of people on both sides of the pit wall, the lethal years have ended. But make no mistake, motor racing will never be "safe." At the 2013 Monaco GP, *Rush* director Ron Howard was asked by NBC Sports Will Buxton about safety issues back in the *Rush* days of the 1970s compared with now. Ron's instant answer was, "Yes, it was more dangerous in the 70s, but you can't tell me *this*—" he swept his arm across the Monte Carlo circuit—"is *safe*!"

We won't, and it's not. But grand prix circuits are no longer weekend killing fields.

An unintended consequence of the throttling back on the dangers is that formula racing these days attracts a different kind of driver. He (and someday soon, *she*) is more a technician, a cool-headed astronaut, driving no longer by the seat of his pants but by the feedback from thousands of points of information streaming from his car to the pits, the garage, even all the way back to the factory in a far-off country. He no longer has to feel everything his car is doing; his in-helmet radio contact will tell him. It may also tell him what to do about it, whether he wants the advice or not.

The changes just keep coming, most of them for the better.

CHAPTER 3

How Racing Has Changed– or Not

What has changed since the late 1970s

A driver used to be the only source of info about what was going on in the car. He'd do the testing and practicing, then dart into the pits, report his findings, watch the engineers and mechanics respond, then dash back out again. Some drivers were far better than others at sensing what was wrong or right. Some teams were quicker to grasp what their driver was reporting.

He's no longer the sole source or even the main source of technical info for the engineers and designers. He's merely one of thousands of bits of info pouring into the team computers during a run. Technology has progressed with the speed of light, to where it almost seems as though the driver is just there to work the levers (hold your fire– there's more on this in the next section).

Safety has strengthened to the point where just one racing accident since 1994[1] has claimed a driver's life. Even major crashes are

---

[1] Jules Bianchi's Marussia crashed in the Japanese GP in October 2014. He never regained consciousness before dying in July 2015.

now survivable, and few inflict lasting injuries.

Today's fans are also technologically light years ahead of the earlier fans. These days they're used to high tech, they speak the language, they're excited by it, they love seeing it in action. They don't need to see Lewis' facial expressions to be a Hamilton fan, they just want to watch the results of the miracles he works down in his submerged office.

The driver is no longer alone in his car; he gets all kinds of info from his pits direct to his helmet, including such occasional advice as, "Try to get around so-and-so ahead of you."

He no longer gets much breathing space between races; he's scheduled for interviews, photo shoots, charity affairs, endorsements, expert panels, car shows, sponsors' events, meet-and-greets, you name it—on top of vital consultations with his engineers, mechanics, team principal, and other team personnel. Precious little time remains to digest it all, even less for contemplation and planning. His social life? Crumbs from the table, whatever's left.

The time crunch by itself does not account for today's driver having few friends inside racing. Back in the day, close friendships developed among the drivers, extending to their wives and children and parents. FI has always been a world unto itself but inside, a closeness prevailed; drivers, competitors, mechanics, managers, they were *family.* The sport slowly evolved into every man and every team for itself, partly because of the rocketing costs. Competition for engines, sponsors, drivers, designers, engineers, etc. grew fierce as the financial stakes grew gargantuan. FI became a cutthroat Big Business with little room for the warm and fuzzy. Nowadays, even the same team often has two opposing factions, splitting the garage into Driver A's team and Driver B's. The atmosphere can range from forced smiles for the camera to downright toxic.

And for what it's worth, grand prix isn't even called grand prix much anymore—it's Formula One or FI.

What has not changed

The goal of every driver since day one is to win races. If he can't win, take second or third. If he can't get a podium finish, then at least earn some championship points. If no points, then just hang on to his ride, which is not easy because a driver's team owner and his cash-bearing sponsors want results.

Another immutable is that no matter the technology, it's still only *his* foot on the pedal, *his* reflexes and heart and strength, and his alone. Ain't nobody else out there wrestling a pig of a car or guiding a rocket.

For every FI driver since day one, winning is his default setting. Anything less than first place means he *lost*. Something didn't work, went wrong, needs fixing. And he doesn't merely dislike second place, or fifth or whatever. He *hates* not winning.

Former FI driver David Hobbs on the telecast of the Hungarian GP July 28, 2013, said that "Every driver on the grid, no matter how far back he is, thinks he can win the race." So although someone so completely dominating as Jim Clark/Michael Schumacher/Sebastian Vettel/Lewis Hamilton "is discouraging," Hobbs said, "still, drivers are optimists."

Are they ever. In the next chapters you'll meet some of them as I knew them.

CHAPTER 4

The Drivers

Amon, Chris

Beltoise, Jean-Pierre

Brabham, Jack

Depailler, Patrick

Fittipaldi, Wilson

Ginther, Richie

Gurney, Dan

Hill, Phil

Ickx, Jacky

Lovely, Pete

Moss, Stirling

Pescarolo, Henri

Redman, Brian

Revson, Peter

Scheckter, Jody

Siffert, Jo

Wisell, Reine

Andretti, Mario

Bondurant, Bob

Cevert, François

Elford, Vic

Ganley, Howden

de Graffenried, E.

Hailwood, Mike

Hobbs, David

Ireland, Innes

McLaren, Bruce

Oliver, Jackie

Peterson, Ronnie

Regazzoni, Clay

Rindt, Jochen

Schenken, Tim

Stewart, Jackie

Bell, Derek

Bonnier, Jo

Courage, Piers

Fittipaldi, Emerson

Gethin, Peter

Gregory, Masten

Hill, Graham

Hulme, Denny

Lauda, Niki

Mosley, Max

Pace, José Carlos

Posey, Sam

Reutemann, Carlos

Rodriguez, Pedro

Servoz-Gavin, J.

Surtees, John

CHRIS AMON
New Zealand (July 20, 1943 – August 3, 2016, Age 73)

Chris was the original hard-luck kid. Not once in nearly 100 tries did he win a championship grand prix. He usually qualified well if his car allowed it, and he did win eight non-championship grands prix. About every ten races or so he managed a second or a third, so he did get some podium glory. He was more successful as an endurance driver, winning the 1966 Le Mans with fellow Kiwi Bruce McLaren, the Monza 1000, the Daytona 24-Hour, and events in the Tasman Series.

His F1 bad luck consisted of constant mechanical breakdowns; replacement on a team by superior drivers suddenly aboard; crash injuries; team finances causing evaporation of promised rides. It just never let up, and when he finally retired in 1976, he had precious little grand prix hardware for his trophy cases.

Upon seeing Niki Lauda's crash in the 1976 German GP, he walked away from the sport. He'd also witnessed the horrifying deaths of Lorenzo Bandini and Jo Schlesser and Piers Courage and François Cevert. Motor racing was killing too many of his colleagues, and Lauda's very close brush with dying tipped the balance. Chris attempted to race in a few more long-distance events, but his heart was no longer in driving and he stopped racing altogether.

He returned home to New Zealand, where he was an honored celebrity. He became an increasingly active and substantial supporter of young drivers trying to climb the racing ladder. He threw himself into the administrative side of New Zealand racing, in raising funds for the Bruce McLaren Foundation, and in new circuit design. There is a Circuit Chris Amon that hosts the annual finale to the Castrol Toyota Racing Series, which awards the Chris Amon Trophy to the series winner. Several of those competitors move on to Europe and F3, where they arrive better prepared because of the racing experiences provided by Amon's many ideas and activities.

Chris was claimed by cancer in 2016. So unlucky in his own career, his efforts bring priceless good luck to young drivers today and well into the future.

Facing a stiff headwind as always, Chris spectates at the 1969 USGP at Watkins Glen while transitioning from Ferrari to March.

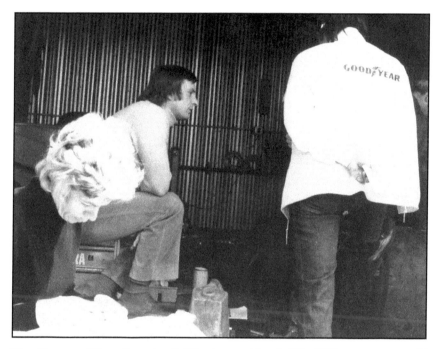

The Questor GP at Ontario, California, on March 28, 1971, was a one-off, two-heat hybrid affair. Here just before qualifying, Chris gets another sponsor patch sewn on his driving suit for another penny in his pocket.

Chris waits to take his Matra out for practice at the first and only Questor GP, where he would finish 4th overall, with Andretti's Ferrari the aggregate winner.

On race day at The Glen, 1972, Amon's lousy luck stayed with him as his Matra finished second-to-last while the Tyrrells of Stewart and Cevert sped off to take the top two spots.

MARIO ANDRETTI
United States February 28, 1940

By the time Mario was 27 years old, he'd already won the USAC (now NASCAR) championship twice. He won the 1967 Daytona 500 and days later the Sebring 12-Hour. He got to drink the milk at the '69 Indy 500. He ended up on the cover of *Newsweek* magazine and in headlines in most Monday morning newspapers. He was so successful in so many American races and he'd attracted so many sponsors that he earned deep into six figures in 1969, a year when the average American salary was just under $7,000. He was a hard charger who never gave up and never gave in.

All this caught the eye of two of the most powerful and successful men in F1: Enzo Ferrari and Colin Chapman of Lotus. Nobody in their right mind turned down a chance to race F1 Ferraris—but Mario did. A full-fledged star in the United States, Mario also said no to Chapman except for a single outing at the 1968 USGP where he took the pole, qualifying faster than such established stars as Jackie Stewart and Graham Hill; who knows how the race would've ended had his Lotus not broken as he was challenging Stewart for the lead.

Mario was so quick and so much a racer that, most uncharacteristically, both Chapman and Ferrari would offer him second chances. This time, he accepted the Lotus offer because by 1969 he felt ready for more than just his one race in Formula One. (His identical twin, Aldo, had quit racing after a second serious crash.)

An established star, financially set, Mario at 29 plunged into the strange world of F1 as a newbie. His early grand prix history is spotty—a few races for Lotus, a few for March. His first full F1 season was 1971 with Ferrari, for whom he promptly won the South African GP. The next years were again sporadic until 1975 when he raced a full season with the Parnelli Jones Ford.

Enter Colin Chapman—again. It was unheard of for him to offer a slot a third time, but what he wanted he usually got, and he finally got Mario. For five seasons the two made a good team, highlighted by Mario's World Championship in 1978, only the second and so far the last American to win the title.

In a stroke of perfect symmetry, Mario clinched his world title at Monza, the track at which exactly 24 years earlier he'd watched his first grand prix. Through a child's dazzled eyes he saw Fangio drive his Mercedes to victory, and on the spot he was bitten by the racing bug that would guide his life. Seldom does fate treat us to such a perfect arc, and Mario today still talks about that Monza connection.

After winning his title, however, his Formula One trajectory faltered. Things went pretty much downhill at Lotus. After a fling with Alfa Romeo in 1981, in '82 Mario drove one last race for Ferrari—at Monza (more symmetry). At age 42, he took the pole and ended up in third place—a podium finish in the final overseas grand prix of his career. He also raced a Ferrari that year in the Caesar's Palace GP, where he was forced to retire. Except for winning the World Championship, though, his achievements in Formula One weren't what he expected or was used to. It was time to move on.

The *breadth* of Mario's success is jaw-dropping. He won races in midget cars, stock cars, endurance cars, Indy cars, F1 cars. Versatility is a characteristic he greatly admired as a kid, so one rejoices over the fact that he then became one of the most versatile drivers in the world. (Fans of Stirling Moss, Dan Gurney, AJ Foyt, and Juan Pablo Montoya can add their names to this exceedingly short list.) Amassing such wide experience, however, constantly stretched his schedule to the near breaking point and opened him to occasional criticism. But as he told Will Buxton in an NBCSN interview aired 11-3-13, "It's amazing how you learn from one discipline to another. There's always something that you learn that's valuable." (But today's age of specialization and virtually air-tight schedules preclude most F1 drivers entering other types of events.)

The *length* of his success is unmatched. From racing on dirt tracks in the late 1950s up through the 2000 Le Mans, he actively raced in *six decades.* In that Le Mans race, he co-drove with the *son* of an early competitor. Mario was 60 years old.

Racing brought him bone-deep satisfaction to be found nowhere else. As he said to Will Buxton, "You never get enough of it." Then he added wistfully, "I never did."

Italy's racing heritage is broad and deep, supported by some of the most passionate racing fans on the planet, the *tifosi*. And if an institution can qualify as a *tifoso*, the Italian government is first in line. In October 2006 it awarded its highest non-military honor— the *Commendatore dell'Ordine al Merito della Reppublica Italiana*—to a racing figure for only the third time in its history. The first time it picked Enzo Ferrari. The second, Carlos Reutemann. The third, it chose Mario "for his racing career, public service, and enduring commitment to his Italian heritage." (Italian-born, Mario became a U.S. citizen in 1964.) From that time on, each man could (and Enzo did) use the title Commendatore.

Mario is still in the thick of racing. He's active in the IndyCar Series, sometimes even driving an odd duck of a two-seater open-wheeled racer, giving a bedazzled prize-winning fan in the back seat the ride of a lifetime. He's the official ambassador for the Circuit of the Americas (COTA) in Austin, Texas. The Andretti Winery in California's Napa Valley is his, as is a chain of gas stations, among many other enterprises.

Mario and Dee Ann were married in 1961, a lifelong union that lasted until Dee Ann's passing in 2018. She and Mario began what has become an Andretti dynasty: Son Michael raced until 2003 and now runs the Andretti Autosport brand and team that counts among its many victories the Indy 500 win by Takuma Sato in 2017. Another of Mario's sons, Jeffrey, raced, as did nephew John, Aldo's son. Michael's son Marco races. John's son Jarett started racing midgets.

Andretti and *racing* continue to be inseparable.

Mario and Colin Chapman are just getting to know each other here at the Questor GP in 1971. It would take seven years for the pair to triumph in a big way, Mario winning the 1978 World Driving Championship for himself and the World Constructors title for Lotus.

Mario and Giorgio Tavoni study the car that Mario would drive to the winner's circle at the Questor GP. Dee Ann Andretti waits in the shadows, the typical role of a racer's wife.

Despite fighting tire problems in the 1972 USGP at The Glen, Mario finished 6th and earned one point for Ferrari. Note the tread on the tires, which had less adhesion than today's slicks.

DEREK BELL, MBE
England October 31, 1941

The genial Derek spent five seasons in Formula One on various teams. In Formula Two he took his Brabham to second place in the 1970 European Championship. But his stellar reputation as a champion came from his long-distance races in such beasts as Porsche and Ferrari.

He and Jacky Ickx formed one of the most potent duos ever to challenge endurance events. Le Mans, the Daytona 24 Hour, Sebring 12 Hour, Monza 1000–Derek won them all, most of them multiple times, many of them with Ickx.

And he seems never to have retired. When he was in his early 50s, he co-drove Le Mans at least twice with his son, Justin. In his 70th year for heaven sakes, he raced a Porsche 962 in the Le Mans, where one of his dozens of competitors was David Brabham, whose *father* Derek had raced against. Talk about endurance!

From my own observations, it seems that the endurance stars like Derek–Jo Siffert, Pedro Rodriguez, Ickx, Brian Redman–have a fundamental calmness about them. Maybe it's the huge amount of patience that's required to succeed in races that go on for hours and hours, patience that's contrarily coupled with lightning reflexes and top speeds.

I always found kindness in Derek. Like most of the drivers, he was civil to those of us media worker bees who were allowed to share the pits. But Derek always seemed more willing to connect as he strode by, making eye contact and flashing a friendly smile.

He spends part of his time in England and part in Florida. Watch for him at historic races and exhibitions, where he'll be the one in the center of any clutch of smiling people.

Derek's racecraft extended to endurance racing with its very different rhythms. He wrote his name large in the history of long-distance racing.

The McLaren of Derek and the March of Peter Gethin, right, shared the 10th row of the 1971 Questor GP, helping to inaugurate the impressive new Ontario Motor Speedway that survived until 1980.

JEAN-PIERRE BELTOISE
France (April 26, 1937 – January 5, 2015, Age 77)

Motorcycles and endurance racing drew Beltoise's interest for several years before he tried a formula car. He won the French F3 championship in 1965 and the European F2 title in 1968. Meanwhile, the French marque Matra put him in their F1 car for the Buenos Aires Grand Prix in 1967 and he won the race; it was a non-championship event so he earned no points, but it was a terrific start.

Ken Tyrrell picked him up as Jackie Stewart's Matra teammate for 1969, and Jean-Pierre drove Matra sports cars in endurance races as well. The latter job led Beltoise to collect some most unfortunate racing baggage. His involvement in the death of Ignazio Giunti during the 1971 Buenos Aires 1000-kilometer race put Beltoise through legal and emotional meat grinders for months and brought about the temporary suspension of his racing license. This was about the time that I was around him, and the freshness of that baggage could no doubt be the reason I never saw him smile.

For 1972 he joined the BRM team and won his only championship race at Monaco that year, driving superbly in a treacherous downpour. After retiring in 1974, he raced in touring car events, mostly for Peugeot. He also did test driving for the Ligier F1 team, again lending his skills to a French effort.

He married driver François Cevert's sister, Jacqueline, and both of their sons became race drivers. At his holiday home in Dakar, Senegal, at the dawn of a new year, Jean-Pierre suffered a stroke and succumbed three days later.

Jean-Pierre alone with his thoughts at The Glen, 1969. That rollbar and a helmet offered scant protection for the human body at racing speeds.

Jacqueline Cevert Beltoise tends to the paperwork for her husband's BRM at the 1972 USGP. So <u>that's</u> what the tires are for . . .

Jean-Pierre checks his balaclava while his BRM Team Manager, Tim Parnell, checks the 1972 Watkins Glen weather. It rained and no BRM made it to the finish.

BOB BONDURANT
United States April 27, 1933

In the middle of the 1960s, the U.S. was well represented in international racing by personable Bob. American Harry Schell was long gone, Masten Gregory was elusive, and Mark Donohue and Mario Andretti had yet to make their appearances.

Bob first made his mark in Corvettes, then Ford Cobras, bringing both considerable glory and letting the world know that Bob was headed for even faster cars. Formula One beckoned and he spent two years racing for Lotus, Ferrari, BRM and finally Dan Gurney's Eagle. He found time to also enter the Can-Am series and endurance events such as Sebring, Le Mans, and the Targa Florio.

A big meaty guy, Bob is outgoing and accommodating. He has an anticipatory air about him, probably a symptom of the business enterprises and projects he always had and still has cooking. His main focus after retiring from the cockpit is his driving school, first in California, then Arizona. His school also offers instructional programs in connection with local fairs, races and special events. Bob consulted on the film *Grand Prix* and taught James Garner to race, infecting the actor with the racing bug in the process. For several years now he's been connected with COTA, the Circuit of the Americas, where the USGP, other races, and special events are held in Austin, Texas.

The year 2013 saw a myriad of year-long festivities to celebrate his driving school's 45th birthday and his 80th. Even bigger milestones were celebrated in 2018, and bravo, Bob!

Bob gave the Formula A Lola of actor-racer Paul Newman a good run in the 1971 Questor GP, but the engine died at the 800-acre track.

JOAKIM BONNIER
Sweden (January 31, 1930 - June 11, 1972, Age 42)

Jo Bonnier's life followed a drastically different direction than what was mapped out for him. Instead of entering the planned worlds of becoming either a lawyer or a publisher, he veered from mental pursuits to the physical challenges of motor racing. He managed to blend both worlds when he brought the patina of his Oxford education and six-language proficiency to a profession involving wheels.

Tall, dark and bearded and with a burly baritone voice, he cut quite a commanding figure. He never settled down with any particular team in FI, instead driving as needed for Lotus, Honda, Brabham and Rob Walker. His single major victory came at the 1959 Dutch GP with a BRM. His own Ecurie Bonnier raced Lotuses and McLarens for the last five and a half years of his career.

In 1963, he became the second chairman of the brand new Grand Prix Drivers Association (GPDA), founded two years earlier by Stirling Moss, its first chairman. Using the weight of his leadership role, Jo joined Stewart and others in the constant push for major improvements in racing safety.

His time in the cockpit in FI gradually diminished as he entered Can-Am events and continued in endurance races. He twice co-drove a Porsche to victory in the Targa Florio. He won the Sebring 12 Hour twice, once with Lucien Bianchi, the late great uncle of the late Jules Bianchi. With Graham Hill in 1964 he finished second at Le Mans, where he returned with a Lola Ford Cosworth in 1972. During that race he and an amateur touched wheels on the high-speed Mulsanne Straight. Jo's car whirled violently off the road and spun into the trees. He was killed instantly.

I remember his being a singular and sophisticated presence in the pits. He was a noted art collector and also ran a gallery, giving FI an extra patina of class. I have a 1972 *Life* magazine photo of him and his wife, Marianne, at home. Displayed behind them is his gleaming

Formula One McLaren, skillfully mounted nose down, engine and all, on their beautiful living room wall. Jo's hand rests comfortably on the left front tire as he gazes at the camera with his usual aplomb and a small smile.

Weeks after publication, he was dead. It was a fitting final image of a man who so smoothly graced two very different worlds.

At The Glen in 1969, Innes Ireland, left, pooh-poohed the safety measures that Jackie Stewart, center, and Bonnier worked so hard to implement. Their disagreements, however, didn't disrupt their camaraderie.

JACK BRABHAM, OBE, AO
Australia (April 2, 1926 - May 19, 2014, Age 88)

Where to start with Jack, whose name is writ so large in the vast world of motor racing? To walk with Jack was to walk with history. Australia declared him a National Treasure in 2012, which racing people recognized decades earlier. When he passed, Queensland gave him a state funeral and in 2017, the Royal Australian Mint issued a Brabham commemorative coin.

A mechanical engineer, Jack and constructor John Cooper revolutionized open-wheeled racing by moving the racer's engine from front to middle (F1) and, later, rear (F1 and Indy). When they wheeled their strange-looking car onto the grids in the late 1950s, they changed Formula One and Indy car racing forever.

In 1962 Jack turned constructor himself and shortly became the first post-war driver to win F1 races in a car bearing his name. So far he's the *only* one to win the World Driving Championship in such a car. (Bruce McLaren won one race in his namesake car, and technically so did Dan Gurney. John Surtees earned six championship points in a Surtees racer.)

Jack was considerate, pleasant, and patient with people and situations. He was very quiet and self-contained, so much so that he would do anything to avoid a cocktail party or a publicity stunt. The limelight was simply not in his universe and he was uncomfortable at such events.

He was every inch the minimalist. There was no wasted motion, no grand gestures as he moved quietly along. Even in conversation, he answered many questions with a simple Yes or No. Right after he'd been to a NASCAR (then USAC) race in Phoenix, I asked him what he thought of it. "I just went for the day." Okaaay . . . And how did you like it? "Well, it didn't rain." Nothing further could be nudged from him, so make of that what you will. Still, he was good company, comfortable to be with, fairly passive unless he was out in a racer doing his job –and then watch out! Gentleman Jack got left in the pits as Black Jack took to the track.

He bonded dirt-track drifting with F1 precision, an alarming combination that carried him to three World Driving Championships (1959, 1960, 1966). His skidding through corners was highly visible; his precision, virtually unseeable. I recall one of his Indy 500 time trials, where colleagues, competitors, spectators and officials were flabbergasted after Jack flew around the track doing his three hot laps and the track announced that all three lap speeds were identical to the *hundredths* of a second. That's precision driving.

After Jack retired from the cockpit in 1970, Bernie Ecclestone soon took over the Brabham team and ran it for the next 16 years. Bernie was also president of the Formula One Constructors Association (FOCA). As early as 1984 Bernie was termed "powerful," and he only grew more so until he ran the whole F1 show through being President and CEO of his Formula One Management company and Formula One Administration. Under Bernie's leadership, the Brabham team won the World Championship with Nelson Piquet in 1981 and 1983. Bernie sold out and moved on at the end of the '87 season. The team struggled through the ensuing years until it finally couldn't pay its bills, and the team that Jack built folded in 1992.

Meanwhile back in Australia, Jack and his second wife followed the racing careers of all three of his sons who became race drivers, a development Jack certainly didn't wish for but nonetheless supported. A Brabham dynasty is now surfacing with the entry on grids of a Brabham grandson. As for Jack himself, he scratched his racing itch by driving in exhibition races—serious races but not for anything but some fun for the pros like Jack, experience for kids just breaking into racing, and entertainment for the spectators. In those events, Jack reverted to bumping and blocking, sliding and storming, which proved that Black Jack was still to be reckoned with. His early dirt-track tricks never left him.

Knighted by Queen Elizabeth II and with stretches of Australian circuits named after him, Sir John Arthur Brabham showed up at special reunion-type F1 events deep into his 80s, as shy of the spotlight as ever but still a key participator.

He not only survived a deadly sport but he wrote his name indelibly in the record books as a triple world championship driver, as the helmsman of a championship team and marque, and as a man who helped to change motor racing forever.

Out on a long walk with Jack, I took this "hero shot" at The Glen in 1969. Wikipedia points out that Perth, Australia, has a whole suburb named Brabham, in honor of this racing legend.

Gentleman Jack prepares for the 1969 USGP where although he qualified back in 18th, Black Jack got busy and finished 3rd.

More inclined to listen than to talk, Jack at the 1971 Questor GP hears what American Indy and USAC (NASCAR) ace Roger Ward, right, has to say.

Jack's long-time chief mechanic, Ron Tauranac, foreground, readies Graham Hill's Brabham for the Questor GP. Ron would take over team ownership until Bernie Ecclestone came along.

FRANÇOIS CEVERT
France (February 25, 1944 - October 6, 1973, Age 29)

François was 22 before he even sat in an open-wheeled racer. Just two years later, he won the French F3 title! By 26, he was on Ken Tyrrell's 1970 Formula 1 team and under the tutelage of Jackie Stewart. In only his second year, François placed third in the World Championship. He also found the time to enter Le Mans, where he and co-driver Howden Ganley took second place.

Except when in his racer, François was always smiling that wide dazzling smile of his. He had dark eyes set wide apart and smile-induced dimples. He was strikingly good-looking and not unaware of it. In addition to driving, he was also a classical pianist, with a preference for Beethoven. Just out walking around he wasn't particularly graceful, but at the wheel he could make an F1 car dance. He could even keep the rocketing Stewart at bay during the heat of battle (and keep him as a good friend afterward).

Driver Jean-Pierre Beltoise became his brother-in-law when that other Frenchman married Cevert's sister, Jacqueline. She has the same dazzling smile (there's just no other word for it) and gorgeous eyes. The four of them, often with the Stewarts, grew close and had many a high time together.

After slumping through 1972, François was having a strong '73 and upon Stewart's retirement was due to become Tyrrell's number one for 1974. The final race of the 1973 season changed all that: at Watkins Glen his life ended violently during qualifying. Chris Amon, Jody Scheckter, and Jackie all stopped their cars and rushed to help François, but it was clearly too late. None of them would ever be able to blot out the horrifying scene.

That race was Jackie Stewart's 100th, a milestone achievement that the team was all set to celebrate. Ken Tyrrell, however, withdrew the team out of respect for their fallen comrade who had been so well placed for success in a future that now would never come.

During the 1972 USGP, Cevert would ride shotgun for his mentor Jackie Stewart and insure a flamboyantly displayed Tyrrell 1-2 finish.

The 1972 USGP at Watkins Glen furnished the high point in a down year for François except for the good chemistry between mentor and protégé.

PIERS COURAGE
England (May 27, 1942 - June 21, 1970, Age 28)

Piers was the wealthy heir to the Courage brewery, able to buy race cars for himself and not wait until he got noticed. In his early twenties he raced various open-wheeled cars, crashing nearly all of them while learning the limits. Eventually he did well enough in F3 to attract the attention of Colin Chapman, whose Lotus became Courage's step up to F2.

From there, Piers at age 25 earned an F1 slot with the BRM team, but he couldn't capitalize on it. For 1968, Piers drove for the private BRM team of Reg Parnell and his son Tim. The same year, Piers' friend from early days, Frank Williams, was assembling his Williams F1 team for '69, and Piers signed on.

He was tall for an F1 driver, and he strolled around with a friendly but reserved smile. He and his wife, Lady Sarah Curzon, were close friends of Jackie and Helen Stewart, and Jochen and Nina Rindt. The six of them shared the delights and struggles of Formula One families. Among them they had a clutch of toddlers, which deepened their bond.

Piers earned two 1969 podium finishes in the Williams Brabham-Ford, but for the 1970 season Frank switched to a De Tomaso-Ford. The car proved heavy and cumbersome despite the use of magnesium to lighten the chassis. In the Dutch GP at Zandvoort, something broke on the car and Piers crashed and burned, the impact killing him instantly.

Violent death was always expected but always a staggering shock in this very small, very elite universe, and Piers' death counted heavily in his friend Jackie's eventual retirement from racing.

Listening to team owner Frank Williams, left, turned out well, as Piers would charge from 9th to finish 2nd at the 1969 USGP. Johnny Servoz-Gavin, background, would retire his Matra.

PATRICK DEPAILLER
France (August 9, 1944 - August 1, 1980, Age 35)

A small, quiet fellow, Patrick raced in FI for seven seasons, a remarkable career length given the rate of slaughter during the 1970s. He loved racing from childhood on and worked his way into F2 when in his 20s. He was something of a bad-boy on the Renault endurance team, but in a March F2 he gained experience at most of the big European tracks.

Ken Tyrrell had been watching him, and when at the end of 1973 the Tyrrell FI team was decimated by Cevert's death and Stewart's retirement, Ken called upon Patrick to be Jody Scheckter's teammate for the 1974 season. Over the next four years, Depailler had several big wrecks but also several excellent podium finishes for Tyrrell. His most prestigious win was the glittering Monaco GP, where in 1978 he beat Lauda, Hunt, Reutemann and the rest of the stellar pack. At this point in the year, the win put Depailler in first place in the World Championship (which Mario Andretti would collect at the end of the season).

For 1979, Patrick went back to a French team, this time to Ligier. A podium finish plus a big win in Spain tied him in mid-season for the world title. But Patrick had a fondness for indulging in dangerous sports off-track as well as on, and in June he was badly injured in a hang-gliding accident that forced him to miss the rest of the season.

The new Alfa Romeo team signed him for 1980, but the year proved exceedingly difficult. In the first eight races, Depailler's Alfa broke eight times. As he was testing the car in preparation for the German GP at Hockenheim nine days ahead, his Alfa broke once again, this time inflicting instantly fatal injuries on the man who had grown up in Clermont-Ferrand, one of France's most fabled racing venues. Just days later he would have celebrated his 36th birthday.

Patrick's Tyrrell finished the 1972 USGP in 7th behind winner Stewart and 2nd place Cevert. The three teammates then drove into the pits side by side, showing off wall-to-wall Tyrrells.

VIC ELFORD
England June 10, 1935

Competing for some 15 years, Vic tucked in a three-year Formula 1 stint, driving for three different teams. He earned eight F1 World Championship points, which was no small achievement in a time when a win brought 9 points, then 6-4-3-2-1.

Primarily a sports car victor and rally champion, he won—*won*, mind you— the Targa Florio, Daytona 24-Hour, Sebring 12-Hour, and six major races at his favorite circuit, the hairy Nürburgring. Of those latter six victories, Wikipedia says that "Only Rudolf Caracciola and Stirling Moss beat that record."

He wasn't called "Quick Vic" for nothing, having set fastest laps at tracks all over the racing world. Porsche was his weapon of choice, and he was theirs. In 1967, he won the European Rally Championship. His come-from-way-behind victory in 1968 at the Targa Florio was one for the ages. Before retiring in 1971, he'd raced in nearly every marque imaginable and had entered nearly every racing series extant, including NASCAR and Can Am.

He lives in South Florida, pretty much the exact opposite of his birthplace of London. He travels the world for personal appearances, programs, speeches, festivals, and so on. In 2015 the Road Racing Drivers Club honored him with the annual Phil Hill Award for outstanding service to road racing.

Not only is Vic a tireless ambassador for racing, he has written three books—one a memoir and two editions of his *Porsche High-Performance Driving Handbook*. Who better for any of them than Quick Vic?

Vic pushed this dark McLaren as hard as he could in the 1971 Can-Am race at Laguna Seca (between Monterey and Salinas, California), but couldn't get it to finish.

EMERSON FITTIPALDI
Brazil December 12, 1946

When Emerson was only 25 years old, he became the youngest driver to win the World Championship. That record stood for 38 years, until the 23-year-old Sebastian Vettel eclipsed it in 2010. Although for 1973 Jackie Stewart in his Tyrrell beat Emmo for the world title, Emmo helped Lotus win that year's Constructors Championship for the third time in four years. The very next year he earned his second driving title.

He stayed on in F1 for six more years, surviving in a blood sport that regularly snuffed out its participants. (Emerson was the lead pallbearer at fellow Brazilian Ayrton Senna's funeral.) His last grand prix was the USGP in 1980, but he wasn't about to retire from racing. He put his money and time and effort and reputation and hopes and expertise into the Fittipaldi F1 race team during the early 1980s.

Emmo and brother Wilson have always been entrepreneurs, from teenhood on. Their VW accessories business was born, flourished and sold before they even got to F1. They work extremely well together and share a relaxed, cool-headed approach to endeavors. It's natural for them to turn those energies to new ventures, and equally natural that those ventures would involve motor racing.

I once asked Emmo what he liked to spend money on. "I always think of the future. I save my money to do new things with different ideas . . . I like to design things . . . good ideas depend on the money." He's smart and creative and tireless and personable—a successful mix no matter the challenge he takes on.

Not every project is successful. After years of struggle, his and Wilson's F1 Fittipaldi team went under. Emerson then spent a dozen years racing Indy cars, winning the 1989 CART championship and the Indy 500 twice (1989 and 1993, the latter when he was 47 years old). He'd probably *still* be racing somewhere today if a bad accident at the Michigan International Speedway in 1996 hadn't ended his driving career as his big five-oh birthday approached.

He travels all over the world, sometimes driving in exhibition races, other times waving the green flag, sometimes manning the pace car. He's Chairman of Motorsport.com., a solid source for news about racing of all kinds. In an interview on the Motorsport.com site, with shining eyes and that Fittipaldi grin he says, "To the day I die, I'll still be in racing." And, "That's my life, that's what I love to do, that's my passion."

Exceptionally well-grounded, he's weathered team failures, marriage failures, tragedies, close calls,[2] disappointments, triumphs, riches, bankruptcy, fame and glory with steadiness and grace. Pressure seldom fazes him. He appears impervious to distractions. Oh, he can get angry, of course he can—but rarely, and only for good reason.

His rock-solid foundation is family. His wife, both parents and his brother Wilson, Jr., were traveling with him when I knew him. They were a cohesive group, and although Emmo and I could get off to the side and he'd give me his full attention, the family usually stayed close by. As a group, they either all talked at the same time or fell completely silent, and it was like being near a tree full of energetic birds.

Patriarch Wilson Fittipaldi must be noted here. Emmo's father was a powerhouse in Brazil, where he was the engine behind what became and remains a frenzy for motor racing there. He helped found the Brazilian Motor Racing Confederation and later the Brazilian version of the Mille Miglia. It was his colorful race descriptions on the radio that transported Brazilian listeners to F1 races around the globe.

He and his wife "Juzy", who died in 2006, had both raced as amateurs in their younger years. When Wilson, Jr., and then Emerson began racing in Europe, the two parents traveled right with them. Father Fittipaldi exuded waves of authority, although at F1 circuits, it

---

2   His luck held once again when piloting his ultralight plane in 1997: At 300 feet, the engine quit and plunged Emmo and his son into a swamp. The boy was scratched up some, but Emmo broke his back. Had they been flying over solid ground, surely both would've been killed.

was soon Emmo who was the center of attention and activity. When father Fittipaldi passed on March 11, 2013 at age 92, all Brazil fell into mourning.

Emerson has had three long marriages. Of his seven children, son Luca started racing when he was five and daughter Tatiana grew up to marry a racer. Wilson, Jr.'s son Christian has been racing for nearly 20 years. In 2017 Emmo's grandson Enzo joined the Ferrari young driver program. In 2018 another grandson, Pietro, entered endurance racing.

Happily, an expanding Fittipaldi dynasty is upon us.

Only a Lotus could draw such rapt attention from, left to right, Colin Chapman, Emmo, Reine Wisell, and mechanic Eddie Dennis at the 1971 Questor GP in California.

This is the quiet but certainly not the calm before the storm as Emmo and Chapman, left, each retreats within himself shortly before the start of the 1972 USGP at The Glen.

Emmo, left, his brother Wilson, center, and Moco Pace form a Brazilian triumvirate at the 1972 USGP at Watkins Glen. For Lotus, Brabham, and March respectively, mechanical woes doomed all three to DNFs.

Emmo plus teammate Ronnie Peterson (not shown) brought Chapman the fifth of Lotus' seven World Constructors Championships. Here at the 1972 USGP, Chapman got the apple, too.

WILSON FITTIPALDI, JR.
Brazil December 25, 1943

Wilsonho was the first of the Fittipaldi sons to be the racing star of the family. He took li'l Emerson along as his general mechanic, runner, and all-purpose buddy. When Wilson won enough Brazilian races to be a big frog in a little pond, the Fittipaldi family packed up and went racing in Europe. However, Wilson had little luck there and soon returned to Brazil. Meanwhile, Emmo found racing in his blood, too, and he went on to pursue his own career. The two brothers complemented each other so well and so completely that as Emerson began to make headway in the rough seas of open-wheeled competition, Wilson re-entered the fray.

By the time I met them in 1972, they were both in Formula One, Emmo driving for Lotus and Wilson for Brabham. Wilson stayed three seasons in FI, then turned to creating the Fittipaldi FI team with Copersucar sponsorship. He managed the team through the 1982 season. He then drove stock cars and sports cars in Brazilian events before focusing his time and energies on managing the racing career of his son, Christian. This third-generation driver raced in FI (earning 12 points in 40 races), Indy cars (he was Rookie of the Year at the Indy 500 in 1995) and NASCAR. In 2013 and 2016, Christian co-drove to victory at the Six Hours of The Glen and at the 2018 Rolex 24 at Daytona, among others.

The Fittipaldi beat goes on.

The future manager of the Fittipaldi F1 team, Wilson is the perfect complement to little brother Emmo. Over half a century later, they're still a great pair.

At The Glen 1972, Wilson crouches by his Brabham while Jabby Crombac, left, here in his iteration as a Swiss journalist, investigates the back.

HOWDEN GANLEY
New Zealand December 24, 1941

Howden Ganley has done it all. He's worked on race cars, driven race cars, manufactured race cars, and helps oversee racing. He's F1's Forrest Gump without the Gump characteristics.

He was once addicted to sailing, as nearly every Kiwi is. But when as a youngster he saw his first motor race, he tacked straight into a whole new headwind. He started entering club races in small cars, then bigger cars in bigger races. His successes built to the point where at 20 he headed to England, where still beats the very heart of motor racing.

Already skilled in welding and general mechanics, he became Bruce McLaren's third employee, 'way back when Bruce McLaren Motor Racing Ltd. hunkered in a crumbling corner of a cavernous old building that housed heavy equipment. Howden helped prepare race cars during the week and raced them on weekends, gaining ground on his goal of becoming a Formula One driver. In 1970 he finished second only to Peter Gethin (also in a McLaren-Chevrolet) in the F5000 series, attracting the powers at BRM. He stepped onto the F1 stage in the 1971 season and at the end of it he was honored with the Wolfgang von Trips Memorial Trophy, given to the grand prix equivalent of "rookie of the year." Two years with BRM and one with Frank Williams brought him 10 championship points, back when a win was worth 9 points, then 6-4-3-2-1. His activities faded to just a couple of races in 1974 and an end to his career as an F1 driver.

Not one to ever leave the world of racing behind, he then paired up with his old roommate Tim Schenken to form the Tiga (TIm GAnley) company. Tiga constructed both sports and open-wheel race cars. From its founding in 1974 to its folding in 1989, various teams and drivers rode Tigas to over a dozen international championships.

In the early 1970s, officially Howden shared an apartment with Tim, but unofficially he was living with his racer girlfriend Judy

Kondratieff, who shortly became his wife. I had seen Judy race her Mini-Cooper many times in the San Francisco region, where she and Howden eventually maintained a home. In April 2007, his beloved Judy died after a long battle with ovarian cancer. Her memorial service was attended by some of Howden's most illustrious colleagues including Sir Stirling Moss and Sir Jackie Stewart.

Early in its history, Howden joined the British Racing Drivers Club, becoming its Director and remaining active in its projects. He also returns sometimes to New Zealand for motor sports festivals, where he's welcomed as a hero.

From being a founding member of the fabled McLaren operation to being an integral part of the BRDC and the often rowdy world of racing politics, Howden Ganley will forever be a part of Formula One in all its colorful history.

With his very first championship F1 race under his belt, Howden enters the 1971 non-championship Questor GP, where he would finish 9th overall.

PETER GETHIN
England (February 21, 1940 - December 5, 2011, Age 71)

Seeing Peter nearly always made one feel better. He was usually upbeat, a big smile bubbling up from inside and he was jaunty, he had style.

His early driving in F3 and F5000 moved him up to the F1 McLaren team for the 1970 and 1971 seasons, always easier said than done. Toward the end of '71, he achieved his biggest moment of glory when at Monza he shot from fourth to victory on the final lap, just nipping Peterson, Cevert, and Hailwood. BRM gave him a slot for 1972, but success would not come and that was essentially his last season in F1.

One could say that death kept handing Peter opportunities. Early in the 1970 season, Peter took Bruce's slot at McLaren right after Bruce's death at the Goodwood circuit. He took Pedro Rodriguez's slot at BRM right after Pedro's death at the Norisring at Nuremberg. It can be a hard "sport" and these were some of its hardest years. But even then teams were big business, and when one driver was killed, no matter the heartbreak, no matter the grief, the next race had to be entered, another driver had to be found, clipped in and sent off.

Too often the dreadful toll and pressures catch up with human endurance. By the time of the USGP at The Glen in October 1972, Peter looked exhausted and had tightened up considerably. He had gained his one big triumph at Monza a year earlier but had endured a zillion retirements in his McLaren and suffered the loss of many friends. After he left F1, he went on to win the Tasman Series Down Under in 1974, and he raced a Lola in the Can-Am series, winning Elkhart Lake in 1977. Climbing out of the cockpit and into management, he headed an F3000 team in the late '80s.

Peter stayed involved in various aspects of racing the rest of his life, including becoming the Director of the British Racing Drivers Club from 2005-2008.

Cancer claimed him on December 5, 2011.

Peter sports a new cap as he and Derek Bell share a light moment at the 1971 Questor GP.

RICHIE GINTHER
United States (August 5, 1930 - September 20, 1989, Age 59)

From his first hill climb in an MG-TC in 1951 through the Monaco GP in 1967, this Californian with the broad smile lived his dream behind the wheel. At first he was just another kid with grease on his hands, a *garagisto* laboring over a used engine in a dark garage. He came up "the old-fashioned way," cadging rides where he could, gaining attention slowly but surely, getting better rides and broader experience. Without money he couldn't buy his way up, so he earned it.

One of his early and lifelong pals was Phil Hill, and the two of them did several memorable Pan-American road races together, Phil driving and Richie his mechanic. In the 1950s, Phil and Richie were right in the thick of the Southern California sports car scene. They took big leaps upward when they joined the racing stable of John von Neumann, a west coast foreign car dealer, racer and entrepreneur. Richie moved into the driver's slot and raced with and against Phil in many west coast events at Laguna Seca, Pomona, the new Riverside Raceway, Santa Barbara, et al.

Here I have to interrupt to mention a gorgeous cream-colored 1956 Ferrari 250 Europa that von Neumann once owned. This beauty became mine and my husband Rodger's for a few magical years in the 1970s. Then the clutch started going. To repair it meant either the Ferrari or food and shelter for a family of three (and we're still not sure we made the right choice . . .). The departed car with its bellowing V12 and alligator-lined doors never left our hearts. To this day we keep a photo of it on a bookshelf, like the family member it was.

Richie Ginther proved to be one of the best test and development drivers as well as racer, and we have Richie to thank for the concept of a rear spoiler. At Monza in 1961, Ferrari handling became a problem. Richie's stint as an Army helicopter mechanic came to mind, and he thought that welding a ridge across the back of the car might better control the unwanted lift the Ferrari was experiencing. Eureka.

In an interview in the January 1960 *Road & Track*, Richie told Murray Roche, "I couldn't care less what my qualifying position is, as long as I can be in the first or second row." Um . . . you and a gridful of other drivers, Richie.

He placed so consistently that he climbed his way into F1, driving two years for Ferrari, then three with BRM where in 1963 he ended up third behind Clark and Graham Hill in the World Championship. In 1965, he won the Mexican GP driving a Honda. That was a high point because the next couple of years saw his driving career wind down, at Honda and Cooper and Dan Gurney's Eagle effort. Richie failed to qualify for the Indy 500 in '67 and that July announced his retirement from racing. It was no longer fun.

He managed production-car racing teams in the U.S. for a while. He bought himself a motor home and toured the U.S., just bumming around, until he built a home in Mexico.

In 1989, the BRM team in England held a reunion, which Richie and his wife Cleo attended. Then they hopped across to France to visit Cleo's family. There, near Bordeaux, he was hit by a sudden and fatal heart attack.

The skinny, freckle-faced kid who loved mechanics and going fast grew into the skinny, freckle-faced Formula One driver who amassed over 100 World Championship points and had a wide grin that could light up a room.

Ten feet tall in Southern California racing history, Richie stands on a Goodyear tire at the 1971 Laguna Seca Can Am.

One of the few SoCal kids to make it to the big leagues, Richie became an F1 regular. Here he plays spectator at Laguna Seca in 1971.

EMMANUEL "TOULO" DE GRAFFENRIED, BARON

Switzerland (May 18, 1914 - January 21, 2007, Age 92)

Born with a silver spoon in his mouth, Toulo raced Alfa Romeos first and then the private Maseratis that he drove for many years both before and after WW II. His first victory was in 1936. His best finish after the war was a fourth in 1953 at Spa, one of the fastest and most nerve-wracking circuits on the calendar; that he was driving a private entry made his achievement all the more remarkable. His racing career spanned some 20 years, until he glided into retirement in the mid-1950s.

Among his next activities were serving as Kirk Douglas' action double during the filming of *The Racers* and managing his Lausanne dealership—the place to shop if you wanted a Rolls or Ferrari or an Alfa. He also organized the 1974 reunion of former F1 drivers at the French GP, said to set the template for such reunions from then on.

His compelling charm kept him in the racing universe as a roving publicist-celebrity for Philip Morris Marlboro, which became a major sponsor of motor racing starting in the mid-1970s. Their European operations were centered in Toulo's home town of Lausanne, making him a natural choice for public relations.

The Baron radiated charm and courtliness. Along pit row he would grandly sweep off his checkered cap to each female. A hearty fellow, he seemed to enjoy everything immensely and with good humor. He'd spend much of race weekend near the outer pit wall, peering through binoculars at whatever cars were coming up-track. His years as a driver left him with a pronounced limp, which he did not try to disguise. He knew everyone, and everyone knew him, and we were always delighted to see him.

He is greatly missed.

Cap at its usual jaunty angle, the Baron leads the way toward the action at the 1972 USGP.

Toulo raced against this fellow's father, Reg Parnell. Reggie's son Tim, right, also a former driver, managed the BRM team here at the 1972 USGP.

Who is that masked man? It's Peter Gethin, listening for some possible racing tips from Toulo before the 1972 USGP.

MASTEN GREGORY
United States (February 29, 1932 - November 8, 1985, Age 53)

Some moments you never forget. My first direct whiff of motor racing came in 1968 when I walked into the bleachers at the Indy 500 qualifying for the first time. The jaw-dropping sound of a racing engine in full song was to me the music of the spheres. And I couldn't wait to see who was creating the sound that flew by faster than anything I'd ever heard that wasn't airborne. It turned out to be Masten Gregory, and his name embedded itself in me as the code word for the unimaginable magic of motor racing.

The "Kansas City Flash" was a character among a whole pack of characters. He forever looked about 15 years old, wore thick eyeglasses, had an impenetrable Missouri drawl and scared the heck out of team managers, competitors and anyone who underestimated him (that means everyone). Made wealthy at 19 by an inheritance from his father and seemingly born to race, Masten would arrive at tracks with ridiculously expensive high-powered racers. At 120 pounds, he looked incapable of controlling a Nash sedan let alone the full-fledged, man-eating sports cars he showed up with.

Then the fun would start. Eyes would pop as this *child* would tear up the course and leave the racing stars in his dust. One can't write about Masten without mentioning a unique driving habit, one that you won't find recommended anywhere, by anyone: When a crash looked imminent, Masten would stand up in the car and jump, juuust before impact. Like Richie Ginther, he refused to wear seat belts, both drivers believing survivability lay in getting away from the car during an "incident." Fear had to simply be missing from Masten's DNA to pull this off time after time. The habit bit him back several times, costing him broken bones and missed events; and it's a good thing he had very deep pockets, because he destroyed any number of pricey cars this way.

After earning his stripes in the mid-50s at tracks around Texas, Nebraska, California and such, he expanded his racing to South

America and Europe. Sports car victories and high placings earned him a privateer seat for the Monaco GP of 1957. Driving a Maserati, he grabbed third place, becoming the first American to earn a podium finish in a grand prix. His F1 career was underway.

For the next eight years, he drove for various teams and amassed a decent number of championship points. But the trajectory of his F1 career headed slowly downward. He returned to sports cars and won Le Mans in 1965 with co-driver and good friend Jochen Rindt in one of Luigi Chinetti's NART Ferraris. At the Indy 500 that year, he started back in 31st and charged into fifth before succumbing to oil pressure problems.

In 1970, his friend Rindt was killed. In 1972, his friend Jo Bonnier. Masten had finally had enough. He retired with his wife and four children to Amsterdam, where, according to Wikipedia, he became a diamond merchant for a while, then a glassware businessman.

At the family's winter home in Italy, this fearless, memorable, daredevil driver died in his sleep.

Apologies. This is my only photo of Masten, taken at the 1968 Indianapolis 500 time trials, back when the qualifying weekends themselves could pack the stands.

DAN GURNEY

United States (April 13, 1931 – January 14, 2018. Age 86)

Raised on Long Island, Dan moved to Riverside, California, at age 17, and his timing was absolutely perfect: Southern California was in the throes of taking automobile racing to sudden and breathtaking new heights. There, his early fascination with automobiles found fertile ground in which to grow. He loved tinkering, modifying, tweaking engines—and then seeing what they'd do. He loved charging around a track against competitors. But he had very little money, and at first, no backers. He bought his own car and paid his own way around the old SoCal tracks like Torrey Pines, Willow Springs, Palm Springs, Pomona, Santa Maria.

His early gritty determination led to 1) offers of try-outs from car owners who were intrigued by his *heart* and 2) flying off the track in a cloud of dust because of it. Time after time, he had to convince possible backers to look beyond his exuberance and see his potential.

Eventually he earned the attention of Luigi Chinetti, who controlled Ferrari in the U.S. Chinetti had his ear to the racing ground, and when he felt the time was right, he sent Dan to Maranello for a Ferrari factory test run. That was the start of an international career that eventually spanned a dozen years and seven teams.

For all his early exuberance, Dan's common sense kicked in as he climbed the ranks of big-time motor racing, and he became a big proponent of racing safety. In that regard, he was the first to wear a full-face helmet (in the 1968 German GP).

Dan was nice to be around. He was usually genial and affable, with an irresistible boyish grin. He made eye contact like he meant it, like he was really interested. He often didn't say much, but you knew he was paying attention. He had a reputation for being a perfectionist. As admirable as that characteristic can be, it probably worked against him more often than not because he didn't always know when to stop tinkering with the equipment.

A friend of my mother's was a friend of his mother's, so I know what a beloved son he was. His dad had been a regular performer with The Met for years and was still singing publicly after he retired from the NY operatic scene. Dan inherited a love of opera, but developed a passion for music of a different kind—that of a racing engine in full song.

After several years of driving other people's cars for other people, he developed his own F1 car, the Eagle, for his All American Racers team. He founded AAR in 1965 with Carroll Shelby, whom he bought out in 1970. They set up shop in Santa Ana, California, with crucial backing from Goodyear, Castrol and Mobil, in years when four engines alone cost $600,000. Aubrey Woods designed the Eagle V-12 under chief designer Len Terry.

Dan and his Eagle made history by winning the Belgian GP at Spa in 1967—the first and so far the only time an American-made F1 car in the hands of an American driver earned World Championship points. (Note that Jack Brabham was the first to earn points driving a car of his own construction, in the 1966 French GP; Dan was second; Bruce McLaren was third, at Spa in 1968; and John Surtees at both Dutch GPs in 1970 and '71 is the fourth and to date the last man to do the same.) From Spa '66 through Monza '68, the Eagle flew high, embedding the name of Dan Gurney firmly in racing history as an F1 constructor and team owner.

There is a gizmo Dan designed dubbed "the Gurney flap," which is a sort of raised rail across the very back of a race car. It increases the downforce on the car without seriously disrupting the aerodynamics. It's up to someone more technically minded than I am to explain how this differs from what Richie Ginther designed for his Ferrari.

As a driver and over the span of his 87-race F1 career, Dan charged to a podium finish every four and a half races, an additional amazing accomplishment.

Dan won races in USAC (now NASCAR), Indy cars and long-distance events. He entered them sometimes as the driver and sometimes as AAR team owner. His versatility rivals that of Mario Andretti and Juan Pablo Montoya, the only drivers to score in all four—count 'em, four—big-league racing series.

A frivolous but delightful legacy of Dan's is the podium champagne spray. After he and co-driver A.J. Foyt won the 1967 Le Mans 24-Hour race, Dan spontaneously shook up the victory champagne and started spraying his colleagues, his team and the press gathered by the podium. From then on, the dousing with the bubbly is a part of big-time racing's podium ceremonies.

Another of his many legacies is the Long Beach (California) Grand Prix. He was a co-founder of that venue and on its board of directors from 1974 til 1998. He launched his elite and revolutionary "Alligator" motorcycle in 2002, creating still another lasting contribution.

Phil Hill . . . Dan Gurney . . . Mario Andretti . . . In chronological order, these are the Big Three that forever pinned America to the FI map. Other American participators like Harry Shell, Masten Gregory, Peter Revson, Mark Donohue, Bob Bondurant, and Sam Posey helped lead the way.

Dan never won the World Championship, but his own American team and his own Eagle marque weigh heavily in the balance of things.

Dan had two long marriages. His youngest son, Alex, became a race driver, and as Dan told *Los Angeles Times* writer Bill Dwyer in a February 2, 2008 article, about Alex, "There's some DNA there, only he's quicker than I was." His son Justin became CEO of AAR in 2011, carrying on the long Gurney involvement with racing.

When pneumonia claimed Dan, Southern California was valiantly fighting deadly wildfires, drought, downpours, and mudslides, devastating Callifornia's landscape. Dan Gurney's passing devastated the motor racing landscape, and his loss hurt the heart of everyone who knew him. His wife Evi received messages from all over the world.

Mario Andretti, upon hearing the news, said of his friend, "He's a world champion. The only thing he doesn't have is the trophy. He was that good."

Dan's name, his exploits, his #48, his marque, his legacy—he leaves it all as the glorious light of a proud past and a beacon for motor racing and racers yet to come.

At the 1971 Questor GP, two racing legends have a friendly chat, perhaps about what fun it is to be an F1 constructor. Colin Chapman of Lotus, left, and Dan of Eagle each wove their marques indelibly into the fabric of Formula One history.

Dan and Colin Chapman observe something fascinating at the Questor GP. Dan was tall for a driver and required a special roof "bubble" when he raced closed-cockpit endurance cars.

MIKE HAILWOOD, MBE GM
England (April 2, 1940 - March 23, 1981, Age 40)

Formula One served as the filling in a motorcycle sandwich for "Mike the Bike." Aboard MV Agustas he won four consecutive world titles and on Hondas four more world titles—*world,* mind you. In the late 1950s and well into the '60s, Hailwood virtually owned the perilous Isle of Man TT races. He was one of the greatest motorcycle racers *ever* and a legend even in his own lifetime.

Off the track, he lived the high life of jet planes, luxury cars, and all the "in" watering holes. He reveled in being a playboy and his sense of good times and fun was highly developed. Despite his wealth and fame, though, he never lost one of his fundamental characteristics—modesty.

But back to racing: If two wheels were so terrific, what challenges might four wheels hold? Mike decided to find out, and his proven winning ways opened the usually very tight F1 door. Reg Parnell signed him to drive his Lotus, which Mike did off and on for three years in the early 1960s. He managed to make time for Le Mans, too, where his best showing was a third in 1969. For 1971-72-73, he joined the Surtees F1 team—and imagine the fund of biker stories those two motorcycle world champions swapped!

The third race of the 1973 season drew the circus to sunny South Africa's Kyalami circuit. On the second lap, Mike's Surtees and Clay Regazzoni's BRM collided, Clay's car exploding in flame. Mike sprinted into the ball of fire and caught fire himself. Doused by a marshal, Mike dove back into the flames, unbuckled the unconscious Clay, and hauled him to safety. Both men suffered serious burns but both survived. For his heroism, Mike was awarded the UK's civilian honor for bravery, the George Medal.

For the 1974 season he moved to the Yardley McLaren team. The elite world of grand prix prized Mike not only for his skills but for his warmth and modesty; he easily slotted into the complex machinery of F1 teams of various styles. But both Mike's F1 season and career ended prematurely in 1974 at the German GP, where he smashed his leg in a huge crash. That put him out of commission for several years. But it couldn't quench his thirst for racing. He returned in 1978, not to grand prix but to his old steeds, the bikes. His legions of fans were beside themselves with delight—even more so when Mike (old enough now to be the father of some of his competitors) won several more races over the next few years.

On the first day of spring in 1981, Mike and his two children drove off to get some fish and chips. A truck driver making an illegal turn caused a horrific traffic accident that killed daughter Michelle instantly. In the hospital, Mike fought for life for two days, but it was one battle he could not win.

His son David survived, and to this day preserves and promotes the memories, victories, thrills, and fun times of his legendary father.

Nearly invincible on two wheels, Mike—here with a stripe on his sleeve, at the 1972 USGP—livened up the place when he gave four wheels a try, too.

GRAHAM HILL, OBE

England (February 15, 1929 - November 29, 1975, Age 46)

Graham Hill came to epitomize The English Racing Driver—direct and amusing, charming and outrageous, and with a mustache trimmed for all occasions. His mane of hair added the British Lion aspect, as did his acid grit, unflagging persistence, and ready bite.

I can still hear Graham commenting in many places and many ways, "The bigger the challenge, the bigger the effort." His effort and his leadership kept first the BRM team and then the vaunted Lotus team in the game. For example, after Jim Clark's death at Hockenheim in April 1968 and then Mike Spence's that May at Indianapolis, Graham took the Lotus employees and F1 team on his back. "Colin Chapman," he told me, "just didn't want to know about racing, which was understandable, so we sort of pressed on on our own, really." What Graham's tenacity and empathy did was bring home the double 1968 World Championship—the Constructors title for Lotus and a second driving title for himself.

His early mode of daily transportation was a motorcycle, the results of which left him with a permanent limp after a mighty crash. His early training was with Smiths Instruments, the results of which was a springboard into engineering, which then helped propel him into motor racing.

The man never drove a car until he was 23 years old—and just ten years later, he was the driving champion of the world! He climbed from welfare to wealthy, from scrounging rides and sleeping in haystacks to filling his trophy cabinets and running his own F1 team.

Formula One was just emerging from its commercial childhood during his years of success in the 1960s. Once when we were discussing this, he said that he didn't have a PR firm, that he had an agent who helped him, but "no one actually looking out for work on that score. I haven't even got a secretary . . . I think probably I have missed out on it all . . . Perhaps I should have made more of the fact when I was World

Champion." (Or after he won that crown jewel of FI, the Monaco race, *five years out of seven*.)

He didn't need any PR among grand prix people. His was a dominant presence. No man was more fair-minded or better liked among his tough-minded colleagues. With his panache and humor, he could be great good company, and all kinds of people flocked around him. He loved to hear people laugh and he had a priceless stock of stories, one-liners and sharp asides. "I like slapstick," he told me, "I like looking at the old films" such as Charlie Chaplin and Buster Keaton. He loved to dance, loved to sing, and was something of an exhibitionist at both.

He was drawn to children and they to him, and he and Bette had three of their own: Brigitte was born in 1958 and Samantha in 1965. In between in 1960 came son Damon, who would become the 1996 World Champion—the only father-son pair to each win the title, until exactly 20 years later when Nico Rosberg joined his father Keke, the 1982 champion. Damon, like Graham, served as president of the Grand Prix Drivers Club, and continues his involvement in FI affairs. Damon was also the childhood hero of five-time champion Lewis Hamilton.

Graham could be wonderful company, but you had to tread lightly. His tongue was his weapon of choice, and he wielded it with rapier precision. A few deft strokes and you were smartly sliced and diced.

The year after his second World Championship in 1968, he suffered a horrendous crash at the USGP at The Glen. In the ER, he jokingly asked the surgeons to please even up his legs, but both were damaged almost beyond repair; amputation was discussed. Eight grueling-gripping-gritty months later, however, there he was, on the FI grid once again, in Rob Walker's privately entered Lotus. He even earned a few championship points that year.

Two further years with the Brabham team brought no further successes in FI, although there was one very bright spot: He won the 1972 Le Mans 24-Hour race, co-driving a Matra with Henri Pescarolo.

That victory put Graham in a league all his own: The hat trick. The triple crown. He had won the Le Mans, the Indy 500 and the World Championship (some consider winning the Monaco GP the third leg of the triple). No one else has ever achieved that, not before and not in the nearly half-century since. Currently Fernando Alonso has made it his goal, and he's two-thirds of the way there, however one counts that third leg.

At a non-championship Silverstone race in May '71–battered and at age 43–Graham Norman Hill captured his final victory, winning the Daily Express International Trophy event. It served as the climax to a long and heroic career that had slid into a downward spiral ever since his '69 accident. His famed perseverance had done him no favors, and his race results were grim and getting grimmer. The DNFs and DNSs and even DNQs were piling up.

As he once told me about his golf game, "If I'm not improving, you know there's something drastically wrong." And in the cockpit, something indeed was very wrong–his legs. They wouldn't, couldn't, didn't come back the way he needed them to. For the umpteenth time in his life he was down. But out? Never. So he formed his own F1 team, Embassy Hill.

As both owner and driver, he led his group through '73, '74, and '75 with a lot of hard work and hope, but without much success. In July 1975, he retired, his driving days finally over, and he turned all the racing over to his protégé, Tony Brise. Tony was a young English driver who'd won an F3 championship before driving for Williams in the Spanish GP and finishing the other nine races of 1975 on Graham's Embassy team.

With *flinty* already Graham's default setting, the disappointments and frustrations of leaving the cockpit and becoming the owner of a non-winning team bubbled ever closer to the surface. Graham epitomized the lion in winter, and his increasing growls reflected this.

At the end of the 1975 season, the team went testing at the Paul Ricard circuit in France. Graham was piloting them all back home again on the wintry night of November 29. In ice and fog, his plane went down near his home field of Elstree, north of London. All those aboard, the heart of the team, were killed–Graham, his designer, his team manager, his two mechanics and the 23-year-old Brise.

The whole racing universe recoiled . . .

Adding to the grief and pain, his family soon learned that whatever insurance he had once carried had lapsed ("I haven't even got a secretary . . ."). The burden of team debts and getting sued after the accident fell upon his wife, Bette, who struggled financially to cope.

But half a century later, Graham Hill—tenacious, witty, popular and a handful–remains a towering figure in the pantheon of F1 racing champions.

Graham's distinctive helmet--white oars on black, a tribute to his rowing days—stands out despite the crowd at the Indy 500 qualifying in 1968.

Graham emerges from the drivers' meeting before the 1969 USGP at The Glen. It was the last time he would smile for quite a while.

Jackie Stewart at the Questor GP explains a point to Graham and the Brabham mechanics. Graham wears the traditional driving suit while Jackie wears the latest fire-retardant fabric.

The lion in the winter of his discontent. Four years after his second world title, the prospects for even another podium looked increasingly grim.

PHIL HILL
United States (April 20, 1927 - August 28, 2008, Age 81)

Any conversation with Phil ranged far and wide and held lots of personal philosophy and sage observations. Words were important to Phil. So were feelings, atmosphere, memories, plans. He was always seething with projects, places to go, things to do.

He was raised wealthy, but his ascent was hard and hectic. Like Dan Gurney, he cut his teeth on the Southern California car culture, entering local races like Pebble Beach and Torrey Pines before Laguna Seca even existed. He won enough races to eventually draw Luigi Chinetti's attention.

The seven years he would spend with the Ferrari F1 team were remarkable—not only because of the notorious team politics but because virtually all of his teammates, one by one, died violently out on the track.

One of those Ferrari mates was Count Wolfgang von Trips, leading to a saga that would follow Phil the rest of his life. Von Trips led the championship race in 1961, with Phil in second place as the flag dropped on the Monza grid. The German aristocrat's Ferrari had the pole but got a very slow start and almost immediately he found himself trailing teammates Phil, Richie Ginther and Ricardo Rodriguez, who was entering his first grand prix. Nipping at von Trips' tailpipe were Jim Clark's Lotus and Jack Brabham's Cooper, the latter soon swooping in front of von Trips. Clark could go deeper into a corner than the heavier Ferrari and on lap 2 the Lotus began to pass. Maybe to block that move but definitely to set up for the Parabolica ahead, von Trips counter-moved. The Ferrari's left rear and the Lotus' right front banged together, sending each car spinning. Clark's Lotus wrenched itself dizzily to an eventual stop in the grass, its driver dazed.

The Ferrari, however, catapulted into a crowd of spectators after fatally ejecting von Trips. Eleven fans were killed on the spot. The racers speeding into the scene miraculously dodged the carnage that included the count's body lying in the road. Four more spectators died shortly in the hospital.

The race was not red-flagged, and the drivers did not and could not know the extent of the slaughter. They raced on and even had a podium ceremony for Bruce McLaren's Cooper in third, Dan Gurney's Porsche in second, and Phil taking the win. Profoundly shaken, Phil quietly pocketed his world championship, then traveled to the count's castle as a pallbearer at his friend's funeral.

Phil clinched his world title at the penultimate race of the eight-race 1961 season without even entering the final event at Watkins Glen. Ferrari chose not to come to the USGP, having already nailed down both the driving title and the constructors title. So Phil Hill lapped The Glen not in style befitting America's first World Champion but only as the honorary race steward, riding in a convertible. (Not to be snarky, but Ferrari affairs more often than not turn out to be, um, different than anticipated, and this is a fair example. Okay, so it's snarky.)

Monza was the high point of Phil's F1 career and his last F1 victory. The next three years were not successful, prompting him to focus exclusively on his endurance career. He'd already won Le Mans three times, likewise the Sebring 12 Hour. After his F1 title, he managed just one more endurance victory, at the BOAC 500 at Brands Hatch in 1967.

He turned more and more to his passion for vintage cars. He owned many himself, including a 1915 Packard and 1931 Pierce-Arrow. He was a top judge at concourses d'elegance, and for years he ran a successful restoration business. I happened to be at his home one day when one of his suppliers stopped by, a fabric dealer. Phil greeted him by name and without referring to any records or lists, Phil pointed to the man's samples and rattled off, "I'll need 30 yards of this and 23 of that; this one comes apart at the seams, and that one's a god-awful color; and 22 yards of this one by the seventh of next month, okay?" Two minutes flat and that was that.

Pianos were another passion. Not just regular pianos, not just player pianos, but intricate mechanical pianos with paper rolls that replayed an artist's performance *exactly,* with every nuance preserved. Phil grew so knowledgeable about the complex mechanisms that he became one of the few in the United States who could repair them.

In 1971, he married Alma, whom he'd met a year and a half earlier. She was a Lithuanian raised in Germany, and she was teaching English and German in an American high school; her daughter, Jennifer, was 11. When Phil and Alma's first child together was born in 1974 (with Phil assisting in the hospital), Phil phoned me to share the news that Vanessa Lora had arrived. The next year son Derek[3] was born into a household lively with pets, for Phil had a special affection for animals. One pet was a large white dearly loved cat named Enzo . . .

Giving back to where he started, Phil became the racing director of the Long Beach Grand Prix Association, where the SoCal car culture thrives seemingly in perpetuity.

For several years Phil battled Parkinson's disease. When I last saw him, his illness was apparent and age was taking its toll.

Alma and Phil with Evi and Dan Gurney formed a foursome that for many wonderful years traveled to races, exhibitions, reunions, etc. They were at the annual Pebble Beach Concourse d'Elegance in 1981, where Gurney was to be honored at a special dinner on August 27. Phil was having a difficult time, but Alma couldn't persuade him to skip the dinner and go to the ER for help; he insisted on being there to help honor Dan. Only afterward did she get him to the hospital, where he died the next day with Alma by his side.

Our first American World Champion was gone.

But never *ever* forgotten.

---

3   Derek became a winning open-wheeled racing driver in the States and in Europe; he's also involved with historic auto racing like his dad was. One of his managers was Brigitte Hill, daughter of World Champion Graham Hill.

The Southern California car scene nurtured Phil, and he more than returned the favor by becoming America's first World Driving Champion.

FI's Renaissance man, Phil embodied passions that ranged from artistic to mechanical, from intellectual to physical, and during one phase of his continual growth, motor racing.

DAVID HOBBS
England June 9, 1939

Across 30 years of big-time racing, David piloted long-distance sports cars, open-wheel F5000, IMSA sports cars, Trans-Am, NASCAR Winston Cup, Can-Am, IROC, the Indy 500 and, of course, FI. He was not only versatile, he was uniformly quick, making him a desirable driver for a variety of top teams. In FI, he drove Hondas and BRMs and McLarens and Lolas.

His earliest driving experiences were equally as varied, ranging from crashing his father's prized Jaguar XK140 to test driving for Jaguar—and crashing. Father Hobbs' automotive skills (e.g., he designed the Hobbs transmission) rubbed off on son David, who early on was tricking out his cars for more and more speed. His story is familiar: First came the local club races, getting noticed, then getting better results and higher notice, then better invitations to bigger races, and up the ladder he went. He carried with him a sort of wry optimism that shines through to this day.

Hobbo's an easy guy to be around. He's funny, compelling and reasonable—an engaging combination. His vast knowledge of racing he accumulated the old-fashioned way, by experiencing it first-hand. During his 50th year, for example, he entered his 20th Le Mans, but he might have felt the ticking of The Big Clock this time because one of his co-drivers was Damon Hill, the *son* of early competitor Graham Hill. David's career spanned from 1959 to 1989, not counting a 1993 Fast Masters Championship race in which he finished 4th in a field of 50, at age 54.

For years, he shared his racing knowledge in front of a TV camera instead of behind the wheel. He covered FI races on the NBC Sports Network and NBC after long service with the Speed Channel and before that, CBS and ESPN. What he shared with TV viewers was cogent and concise, which several former drivers can do, but he spiced things up with unique Hobbs stiletto asides and witty judgments.

When he was selected as Grand Marshal for the 2014 Rolex 24 Hours at Daytona, his many friends and colleagues cheered, "About time!"

He did Steve McQueen's high-speed driving in the film *Le Mans*, and he shows up in *Cars 2* as David Hobbscaps. Claims to fame, both of them.

In between his worldwide TV traveling and what-not, Hobbo finds time to run a very successful Honda dealership in Glendale, Wisconsin. He and his wife Margaret raised two sons, Guy and Gregory, who weren't immune to the racing bug. (One wishes for a Hobbs named Calvin . . . although that one is spelled Hobbes.) From Florida, Wisconsin, England, and other spots around the world, David and Margaret now follow the race-driving career of their grandson Andrew.

To fill in the lively details, see his 2018 autobiography, *Hobbo. The Autobiography of David Hobbs, Motor Racer, Motor Mouth,* co-written with Andrew Marriott and with a Foreword by long-time racing and media buddy Sam Posey.

A welcome and familiar face as a TV race commentator, Hobbo was just as welcome as an all-around driver, such as here at the 1971 Questor GP in Ontario, California.

DENIS HULME, OBE
New Zealand (June 18, 1936 - October 4, 1992, Age 56)

You can take the boy out of Te Puke, but you can't take Te Puke out of the boy. Denny never came to grips with what he felt was all the "nonsense" that surrounded him as a celebrity, and he forever resented the hard fact that people wanted his time and attention because he was a World Champion F1 driver, not because he was Denny Hulme from Te Puke.

When he started racing in New Zealand, he preferred driving barefoot, the way he drove his dad's trucks on long hauls. By the time he was 23, he'd earned a place on the Cooper junior teams in Europe and raced mostly with his shoes on. Jack Brabham took him on as a mechanic in 1961 because Denny had years of fixing the trucks in his father's business. At a maddeningly slow pace, Jack let Denny race his Formula Juniors in more and more events, with Denny doing the maintenance himself. Poles and solid finishes finally convinced Jack to gave Denny F1 rides in '64 and '65, making him Jack's second in '66. For 1967, Denny went out and beat his boss and everybody else for the World Championship.

Fellow Kiwi Bruce McLaren wooed Denny onto his team for '68, and for the next seven years Denny worked not only the F1 races but Can-Am events with their thundering 1,000 horsepower machines. Denny's #5 and Bruce's #4, both of them painted a memorably bright papaya orange, alternated winning the Can-Am title.

The first time I met Denny, I had a tough time persuading him at the 1969 USGP at Watkins Glen to do my first interview with him—even though I had arranged it well ahead. He growled that he doesn't talk to the press, that he had nothing good to say about any of us, and on and on. He folded his great arms belligerently and just stared down at me.

I did the only thing I could do: I talked him into it. And once he got to chatting, this stubborn, bellicose bear turned into a shy teddy bear, mumbling and grinning and fidgeting a lot. After a while, he grew more comfortable and conversation flowed a lot easier. For both of us.

After that first go-round, we became good acquaintances and had many relaxed chats. However, his resentment of the media just never quit and he carried a lifelong grudge.

1970 was a black, black year. Denny planned to enter his fourth Indy 500 and was on the track for the May practice sessions. He crashed and his hands caught on fire from the flaming fuel. The methanol flames were invisible, so fire marshals passed him by for the burning car they saw ahead of them. Full recovery was not possible, and his hands and wrists bothered him forevermore. In June that same year, Bruce was killed testing the Can-Am McLaren at Goodwood. Denny somehow dug deep and pulled the shattered team together. He wrote me his feelings about Bruce's loss and I quote it in my book referenced below, pp. 182-183. The next May found him and the team back in Indiana for what was his last Indy 500; two-thirds of the way through, his car broke down.

In 1972, I sent an early draft of the Hulme chapter of my *Road & Track* book, *The Grand Prix Champions*, to journalist Eoin Young because Eoin was very close to Denny and would spot any missteps. Eoin wrote back with brief positive remarks. He then adopted my description of Denny as a bear. In Eoin's next *R&T* magazine report, he made the first published mention of what was to become Denny's nickname: The Bear. I chose it because it fit in so many ways: Denny loved to sleep, long and hard; he allegedly was nearly impossible to wake up; and he was often surly and irascible. Plus, even as big and beefy as he was, when he moved, he really moved; he didn't make a big production of it, but in the blink of an eye he'd be gone.

In F1, successes came along occasionally over the next few years, but not often enough for The Bear. His good friend and teammate Peter Revson beat him for the 1972 Can-Am title. Early in 1974, Peter was killed at the Kyalami, South Africa, circuit. That season Denny retired in five of the 15 F1 events and finished seventh in points. At the final race in Watkins Glen, he literally walked away from the sport and flew home to New Zealand. There, he raced production cars, touring cars, and—back where he started—trucks.

He and his Kiwi wife, Greeta, had two children, Martin and Adele. Tragedy struck the family in 1988 when Martin died in a diving accident.

At the wheel of a BMW in the Bathurst 1000 in Australia in October 1992, Denny radioed that his vision was blurring. His car veered off the road, grazed a wall and stopped. When track marshals arrived, Denny was still strapped in his car, dead of a heart attack. Had he been given a choice, this might be exactly the way The Bear wanted to go—in his beloved part of the world, alone at the helm of a race car.

A don't-fence-me-in personality, The Bear enjoys the October sun at the 1969 USGP.

In F1, Denny drove only for antipodal teams. Black Jack and The Bear made a Down Under team at The Glen, 1969.

A typical example of being alone in a crowd, Denny and Team Manager Phil Kerr reflect worries about their 1969 car at the USGP, and rightly so. It broke right at the start.

Smooth and sociable when he had to be, Denny would rather put his feet up and snooze. He drove his McLaren to 3rd overall here at the 1971 Questor GP.

Protecting and warming those hands he burned at Indy the year before, Denny awaits his Can-Am car at Laguna Seca, 1971. His hands never fully healed.

JACKY ICKX
Belgium January 1, 1945

Victories in motorcycles carried Jacky, like so many other FI drivers, into four-wheeled territory. He was only 22 when he captured a seat in Ken Tyrrell's Matra, but it took another two years before Ferrari invited him aboard for the whole season. He stayed with the *scuderia* for three years and Lotus for two, with sporadic action for several other teams.

In the deadly era when one out of every three FI drivers was killed, Jacky raced 13 seasons at the top, from 1967 through 1979. Those were hard years though, pummeling him with injuries from broken bones to severe burns.

The Ring was his favorite circuit, Jacky trading wins there with Jackie Stewart, one or the other victorious from '68 thru '73 (except for the '70 GP held at Hockenheim after drivers boycotted the Ring for safety reasons; Jochen Rindt won that one).

Jacky left a major mark on endurance racing by winning, among other big races, the Le Mans 24 Hour; there, he ground out victories *six times* over *three decades* ('69, '75, '76, '77, '81, '82). Three of those victories came with Derek Bell co-driving. Jacky became a long-distance legend alongside Phil Hill, Jo Siffert, Derek Bell and Pedro Rodriguez.

Whatever the type of car or course and starting early in his career, Jacky could win races in downpours. Whatever special skills are needed to successfully take one top driver through torrential rains or slick pavements while all around him other top drivers are crashing, Jacky had them. Throughout his long career, he was classified as that rare driver, a *regenmeister*.

His father Jacques was a motor sports journalist who took his young son to many of the races he covered. Young Jacky's experiences well may have helped wire him for patience with the media later on.

I've seen him remain gracious with, shall we say, *thoughtless* reporters and photographers, when other drivers would have rightly lashed out (truth be told, however, he was not noted for being conspicuously gracious to teammates).

Brussels remains his home, where he lives very comfortably on his shrewd business enterprises. He's still handsome, still personable, and still very much a celebrity, so he's still subjected to the weird rumors and gossip that swirl around the famous.

His family illustrates the truth of the apple falling close to the tree: His daughter Vanina is also a racing driver in both open-wheel and sports cars. He himself remains active in various racing activities, mostly backstage.

In the record books, though, he'll always be front and center.

Despite retiring his Brabham at The Glen, Jacky retained his 2nd place in the 1969 World Driving Championship.

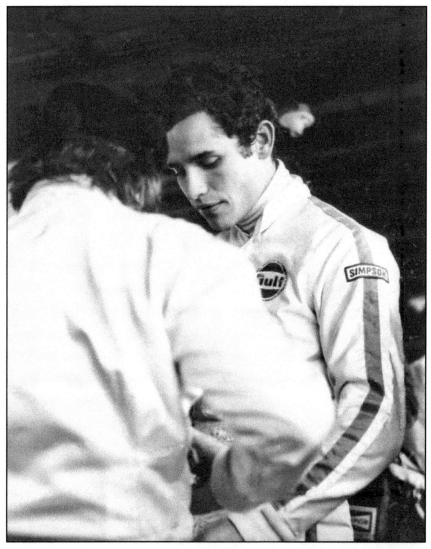

Absorbed in something with Jackie Stewart at the 1969 USGP, Jacky would shift from Brabham to Ferrari for 1970. Of his six Le Mans victories, three of them came with Derek Bell co-driving.

Jacky confers with Giorgio Tavoni near the Ferrari Jacky would drive to 11th place in the unorthodox Questor GP in California.

Helmet technology strives to progress as fast as everything else in F1. While checking his equipment before the 1972 USGP, Jacky gives his visor special attention.

INNES IRELAND
Scotland (June 12, 1930 - October 22, 1993, Age 63)

"Enthusiastic" is far too tame a word to describe Innes Ireland. He lived life with great gusto and verve, and one never knew quite what he'd do next.

His rise was very fast. At age 21 he was a mechanic for Rolls Royce. By 25, he was driving on Colin Chapman's Team Lotus. How did that happen? In true Innes Ireland fashion, his path was unique. Drafted at 22, he did two years with the King's Own Scottish Borderers as a parachutist (a clue, a clue, although he claimed he was drunk when he signed on for *that*). Discharged at 24, he returned to his mechanic's trade and entered a few rallies here and there and the occasional club race. Nothing special about that—except his driving. He won events driving with such skillful abandon that People Who Count took notice. A £500 retainer from Chapman and he was on his way in F1.

In his very first grand prix, the 1959 Dutch, he finished fourth. It was a great start to a career that looked bright as blazes. In 1961, despite still recovering from injuries sustained at Monaco, Innes won the first USGP at Watkins Glen, also becoming the first Scot to win a championship grand prix. But that was as good as it got. He couldn't be tamed, and team leaders couldn't predict what he would do or say. In addition, his driving somehow hit a plateau and he was never able to break free of it, not in his seven full seasons of F1. There would be no more wins and precious few points or podiums.

After he retired, he spent six years captaining a fishing trawler in the Irish Sea, then turned to a less physical occupation. Writing for several motor sports magazines, he proved to be an excellent journalist and, later, an uninhibited TV sports commentator.

He had three children—a son who tragically died in 1992 and two girls—and eventually three wives. (In the very small elite world that is Formula One, it's not a stretch that his second wife had been World Champion Mike Hawthorn's fiancé when Mike was killed.)

Innes was a rowdy character, very well-liked by friends and colleagues, but by team owners not so much because of his independent streak and unpredictability. Self-discipline was not one of his strengths.

In the end, the pranks and chaos gave way to deadly cancer, which snuffed out one of F1's liveliest fires.

Two Scots wage an intense conversation at the 1969 USGP. The grand prix career of the unbridled Innes was colorful and promising, but he proved too rambunctious for even the F1 circus.

NIKI LAUDA
Austria February 22, 1949

Everyone has pluses and minuses, and in Niki Lauda, both are on huge display.

On the plus side, he is safety conscious and promoted safety improvements to the benefit of all. Twice he tried to organize race boycotts over safety issues: He succeeded in South Africa, where he and other drivers brought the track to its knees; his efforts failed at the Ring, where he then crashed and paid an enormous personal price.

He won the World Championship three times—with Ferrari in '75 and '77, and with McLaren in '84.

Austria issued a postage stamp in his honor.

Film director Ron Howard made his and James Hunt's story into the terrific 2013 movie *Rush,* which should be in every fan's film library.

He has owned and managed several airlines—Lauda Air, Niki, Laudamotion. He's licensed as a commercial pilot and occasionally takes to the cockpit (hello, John Travolta).

He has made gritty moves that even Superman might hesitate to try. Such as returning just six weeks after suffering severe burns (at the 1976 German GP) and then, scared to death, coming in 4th at Monza, no less. Such as choosing not to undergo more surgeries on his head and face (he's just glad to be alive, a fact he credits solely to driver Arturo Merzario, who plunged into Niki's flaming cockpit, unclipped him and dragged him out). Such as dropping out of a race (Japan 1976) in which he could have clinched another world championship but retired because he felt the rainstorm conditions were unsafe.

On the other hand, Niki does not always play especially well with others. He's fought with team managers, team owners, teammates, track management, Ferrari, Ford and family. The first time he retired from F1, he was on the 1969 Brabham team and he quit mid-season—suddenly—during practice—by telling then-owner Bernie Ecclestone that he simply no longer wanted to race (but obviously changed his mind later). There weren't many teammates that he didn't resent and/or dislike. After he retired from driving and stepped in to administratively help lead the Jaguar team in 2001, harmony was in short supply. His relationship with Ford was not a success.

Back in 1972 when I first met Niki, he was mousy and quiet and seemed alarmingly frail and unsuited for the frantic and often boisterous life of a grand prix driver. However, he was then at a dreadful low point in his life—drowning in debt and driving a March in one of their bleakest years. But somehow, some way, he would shortly pull his life together, throw off the Clark Kent suit and go on to become a three-time world champion, a survivor of immense inner strength and an enduring force in F1 affairs.

On the family side, over a period of 28 years and two wives, Niki has four sons, one of whom has a twin sister. His son Mathias is old enough and Lauda-enough to have become a race driver like dad.

For several years now, Niki has been the non-executive chairman of the Mercedes F1 team. He helped lure Lewis Hamilton away from McLaren in 2013, and Lewis promptly brought Mercedes three of their next four (so far) Constructors titles (Nico Rosberg reeled in the 2016 title) and Hamilton his World Driving Championships #2, #3, #4 and #5 (so far). Niki helped ease Mercedes' transition in team principals for 2014. He's heavily involved in negotiating financial terms between the Mercedes board and first the F1 czar at the time (the very same Bernie Ecclestone he'd walked out on 45 years earlier) and more recently the new owner of F1, Liberty Media. And, oh yes, Niki owns 10% of the Mercedes F1 team.

He could be mellowing, but don't bet on it; it's more likely that at Mercedes he has finally found the right fit. *F1 Racing* magazine counts him as one of the most powerful people in Formula One (May 2017 issue, p. 41). Whenever and wherever he is involved, Attention Must Be Paid.

He came *this close* to losing his life—again—in August of 2018, this time to a lung infection that came within days of killing him and required the transplant of two new lungs. But he powered his way through it—again.

Savvy, surviving and scrappy turned out to be a winning combination for Niki. So stand by for what are certain to be further developments in the always intriguing and vivid saga of triple World Driving Champion, Mercedes F1 force, and general mover and shaker, Niki Lauda.

Looking like a gust of wind could blow him away at The Glen in 1972, Niki's iron will, great courage and snappy smarts would turn him into a heavyweight power in the world of F1.

Fierce competitors between the green and the checkered, Niki and Ronnie Peterson—two of the fastest drivers in F1—collegially discuss who-knows-what at The Glen in 1972.

PETE LOVELY
United States (April 11, 1926 - May 15, 2011, Age 85)

Anyone who followed American West Coast racing saw Pete Lovely tearing around Laguna Seca, Palmdale, San Francisco and points north and south for over 50 years. From 1947 until he hung up his driving gloves in 2009, Pete was a regular on the circuits. Schedule an event on road or track and Pete popped up on the grid.

Born in Montana and raised in Seattle, Pete settled in Tacoma where he owned and ran a Volkswagen dealership for 34 years. He was an aviation mechanic in WW II, and he applied that knowledge creatively to racing cars. For example, he put together a Cooper with a Porsche engine (his famous "Pooper") with which he won an SCCA F-Modified National Championship in 1955 and again in 1956. By 1959 he was racing an F2 Lotus with an F1 engine. He was one of the last privateers in F1, qualifying for seven races over a 12-year period. His best finish was seventh in the 1969 Canadian GP, nearly winning what would've been his one and only championship point, except that until 2003, points went to only the top six places.

It's not often that local races include an honest-to-Pete Formula One driver, but what else is a driver to do who retires from F1 at 45 and still has the itch? As more years piled on, however, Pete focused more and more on events for vintage and historic cars. Not only that, but he added a car restoration business to his dealership.

He won no world driving title points, he never won at Le Mans, but he happily raced in F1, international sports cars, SCCA and classic events. The man purely loved cars and racing them.

Pete immersed himself in the world he so dearly loved, such as here at the 1972 USGP. All cars great and small, old and new, exotic and not so much, were his life.

BRUCE McLAREN
New Zealand (August 30, 1937 - June 2, 1970, Age 32)

It's easy to get caught up in the big-time operation that is today's McLaren—over 5,000 employees, scores of victories, decades of history. It's easy to forget that it was all started by just one guy in only his mid-twenties who'd already had a dozen years' experience fiddling with cars and was an engineer and designer.

Bruce was both meticulous and demanding in his work, never willing to settle for craftsmanship that was "good enough." He was tireless and dedicated in his quest to get ever-better results from a car, to improve-improve-improve. It was just natural, then, that he'd have to try out what he wrought. In local races, he got so good that he found himself at age 21 racing the circuits of Europe as the recipient of New Zealand's very first "Driver to Europe" program. There, he caught the eye of Jack Brabham and John Cooper, and Bruce was on his way as a driver in Formula One.

At age 22 and three months, he became the youngest winner of a grand prix on December 12, 1959, in the USGP at Sebring, Florida. Lewis Hamilton nearly equaled that record when at 22 and five months he won the 2007 Canadian GP at Montreal. Bruce's record stood for nearly half a century, until Sebastian Vettel surpassed it on September 14, 2008, at the Italian GP at Monza at age 21 and nine weeks. *That* record stood for eight years until barely-shaving Max Verstappen won the Spanish GP on May 15, 2016, at 18 years and 227 days.

Bruce first raced in Europe in 1958, then joined the Cooper team in '59. Within a few years, he felt ready to create his own race car. McLaren Motor Racing Ltd. was founded on September 2, 1963, and three years later an F1 car emerged from his garage, the marque making its official debut at the Monaco GP of 1966. That was the second instance in Formula One of a driver and car bearing the same name (Brabham was the first and Surtees the third; Dan Gurney would've been in this elite group if he hadn't named his marque Eagle).

Among Bruce's engineering innovations were the "nostrils" that race cars still use today to reduce aerodynamic drag.

Fielding an F1 team requires tons of energy, skill, money, time, you name it. But the enterprising Bruce eyed the new Canadian-American racing series and came up with what it took to field a Can-Am team as well. From 1967 through 1972, the papaya orange McLaren-Chevrolet Can-Am howlers dominated that series, with Bruce and countryman Denny Hulme winning nearly everything in sight.

Concurrently, Bruce was also racing full-time in F1, where he collected a massive number of championship points, although never the world title itself. Oh, yes, and there were his Le Mans entries, too, for Ford. He and Chris Amon led the 1965 race before breaking, and together they won the marathon in 1966, as excitingly described in A.J. Baime's book, *Go Like Hell*.

The 1970 F1 season opened, and during the break between Monaco and Spa, Bruce was testing his Can-Am car at the Goodwood circuit in England. June 2 was the Tuesday before the Belgian GP. At speed out on the straight before Woodcote, the rear body panel worked loose, destroying the car's aerodynamics and sending it hurtling off the track. The catastrophe was over in moments, and a profound force in automotive engineering was lost forever. Whatever innovations, fresh ideas, and inspired creativity Bruce would have come up with, were snuffed out on that dark day.

Shaken and numb, Denny Hulme went to the factory, pulling things together despite his own grief. American team member Teddy Mayer took over the team along with Tyler Alexander and Phil Kerr, and McLaren F1 cars soldiered on in F1. But success drifted off and by 1980 the team was gravely struggling.

Enter Ron Dennis.

A history of the McLaren empire after Bruce's death would require a book as thick as a brick. But it would be well worth reading for all the razzle-dazzle, seven World Driving titles, *ten* World

Constructors titles, tumbles down the rabbit hole, boardroom in-fighting, dark days, overseas support, soaring successes, and legendary names like Senna and Prost, Alonso and Hamilton, Lauda, Newey, Marlboro and Bahrain and hypercars. The name of Ron Dennis would arguably gleam brighter than any of them because it was Ron who crafted the decades of McLaren renown. He also fostered the building of the spectacular McLaren Technology Centre in Woking, Surrey, which opened in 2004 and still looks futuristic. A man of exceptionally strong positives and negatives, Ron exited McLaren in the autumn of 2016, but he left behind an automotive giant befitting Bruce's legacy.

McLaren celebrated its 55th anniversary in 2018. The marque has entered well over 1,000 grands prix. Lately, however, one minute the McLaren F1 team teeters on the brink of implosion, the next on its way back to days of glory.

That doesn't make it unique: the world of Formula One holds stunning quicksilver highs and catastrophic lows for all who dare to enter. By its sheer longevity, McLaren has endured more than most, alongside Williams and Ferrari.

What Bruce would think of the many iterations and gyrations of his namesake business is fuel for thought. But we will never forget that it is Bruce himself and his constant striving to make things better, faster, and stronger who stands at the start and heart of all things McLaren.

At the 1967 San Francisco International Auto Show, Bruce accepts his Can-Am Championship trophy. John Surtees (1966 champion), middle, and Denny Hulme (future 1968 and 1970 champion), left, share the moment from their seats on stage.

Bruce and Team Manager Teddy Mayer exchange thoughts at The Glen, 1969, where Bruce would qualify 6th but had to retire in his last USGP.

Bruce's legacy cannot be overstated. Half a century after he sprang the McLaren marque on the world, his brand still carries enormous prestige.

MAX MOSLEY
England April 13, 1940

The resilience Max developed as a youngster dragged by his famous family from England to Ireland to France and back served him well as he fought his way to the top of FI and beyond. Throughout a highly unusual life[4] he battled the media with one hand while with the other hand hurtling out of airplanes as an Army parachutist, then coursing his way through Christ Church at Oxford in physics, followed by becoming a barrister.

Along the way, he got a whiff of motor racing and instantly succumbed to it. He taught law classes at night until he and his wife, Jean, could scrape up enough money to buy him his first race car, a Lotus. On race weekends, he was finally what he wanted to be—a race driver, albeit it one with rather unique qualifications.

From May of 1961 when he saw his first race, at Silverstone, won by Stirling Moss in a downpour, through the next half century and counting, motor racing has been Max's life. Driver, legal advisor, team owner, negotiator, rule-maker—each job led to the next one until he was at the top of the heap, and his journey serves as a monument to perseverance, patience, and vision inside the steamy greenhouse of an elite, closed world.

During his earliest years of racing, Frank Williams was his mechanic (a good illustration of how intricately interwoven is the world of Formula One). Max retired in '69 from driving but not from racing, for he was already hip-deep in forming the **M** in the brand new March FI Team along with **A**lan **R**eece, Graham **C**oaker and Robin **H**erd. Max handled the legal and commercial side of the team. March shot up to third in the Constructors championship not just once but twice—an enormous accomplishment for a newbie and one that wasn't a factory team. Behind those bright achievements, however, stood

---

4   See *Max Mosley, The Autobiography—Formula One and Beyond*, Simon & Schuster, 2015

Max as he plunged headlong into the nightmare struggle to keep the team afloat financially.

It was at this point in his life that our paths would cross. I'd see him around the pits and paddock, this red-haired man who walked on the balls of his feet like a high school athlete. He was tall and lean and *serious*. Even the drivers, who knew they could and probably would die tomorrow, could laugh or horse around with their colleagues. But I never once saw Max even smile—an understandable condition, I think, given that he was ever trying to keep his whole team from going under.

If the March team were a private family, you'd say they were living hand-to-mouth, paycheck-to-paycheck. Securing sponsorship and funds was a never-ending slog, and Max carried the load from '69 through the '77 season when he finally withdrew from the team, and the team then withdrew from FI.

Next, Max put his legal expertise to work for what was eventually called the Formula One Constructors' Association (FOCA) headed by Bernie Ecclestone (who'd bought the Brabham team). When Max left there five years later in 1982, he'd helped put together the Concorde Agreement, which Wikipedia describes as "essentially giving FISA (motorsport's world governing body) control of the rules and FOCA control of promotion and television rights" of Formula One.

After that, Mosley took a four-year break from motor racing affairs. He'd been raised in a politically active family and he now got involved in English politics, both helped and hindered by the notoriety of the family name.

By this time, Max had known Bernie Ecclestone for over ten years, and it was Bernie who drew him back into FI in 1986, when Max continued his climb to the very top of FI politics. He became president of FISA in 1991 and by 1993 was elected to his first four-year term as president of the FIA, the parent body of FISA.

Tumultuous stretches lay ahead that included sex scandals,

breakaway teams, financial thrusts, threats and counter-threats, stand-offs, compromises, legal maneuvers, negotiations, bluster and wisdom. Big-time racing gets complicated, to say the least.

Through it all, Max achieved notable changes in the sport of Formula One and motor racing worldwide. He pushed for a cap on FI expenses to try to keep exorbitant costs under control. He advocated for more green technology in racing. He exercised damage control when tobacco sponsorship went up in smoke. He played a crucial part in supporting the groundswell for better safety awareness and equipment in FI, promoting such safety measures as the HANS (**H**ead **A**nd **N**eck **S**upport) gizmo and working closely with the soon-legendary Dr. Sid Watkins, whom he appointed as the FIA safety director.

In 2009, Max's fourth four-year FIA term ended and he chose not to run again. Jean Todt, ex-Ferrari Executive Director, slipped into Max's very hot FIA seat as president and remains there today.

That same year, Max's son Alexander, 39, lost his struggle with drugs and depression. Max and Jean have a second son, Patrick, and the whole family finds itself in the glare of the media spotlight always turned upon Max. He attracts attention partly because he continues to financially and publicly heavily promote causes dear to his heart. He lends his considerable weight to such issues as tighter press regulation, feeling that he has fallen victim to the media over the course of decades. And having been hacked, he actively supports fellow victims as they work together to bring hackers before the law.

As he has done throughout his lifetime, he continues to fight on all fronts with clout, perseverance, and plenty of panache.

Max enters his March pit at the Questor GP of 1971, while something outside attracts Ronnie Peterson's attention.

The chill creeps up on Max and Chris Amon at the 1972 USGP. Both struggled down in the trenches for years, but each finally moved on to shine in other areas of racing.

STIRLING MOSS, OBE
England September 17, 1929

Some people talk. Some people think. Some people act. Sir Stirling Moss excels at all three—usually at the same time and at top speed. He can talk, oh, can he talk—on any topic, anywhere, with anyone, any time. He never stops planning, plotting and pondering. He's a buzzing bee of activity, always moving, always busy. Part of all that is fueled by his alarming energy and part by his acute discomfort with inactivity. The sum total has propelled him to hero status across half a century and most of the globe.

He was an accomplished equestrian before he traded four legs for four wheels. His distinctive white helmet was simply his polo hat that was handy at the time. His first grand epreuve was the Swiss GP of 1951, during such heavy rain that he had to use one hand to hold his helmet on. Then on the final lap his HWM ran out of fuel and he coasted over the line, losing one place and ending up eighth. That was the inauspicious start to his quest for the World Driving title, and it rarely got any easier. What with engine failures, wheels falling off, parts breaking, he didn't get his first championship points until three seasons later, when he willed his independent Maserati into third place in the 1954 Belgian GP and earned his first four title points.

From that year on, his quest turned into an unbelievable streak of just-misses: Four seasons in a row, 1955-1958, he ended up in *second* place, three times losing out to Fangio and in '58 missing the title by one point to Mike Hawthorn (and that single little point was virtually a gift from Stirling himself; for details, check the Portuguese GP). In '60 and '61, he placed *third*. That's how close he came, year after year after year after year.

What was the problem? Mostly it stemmed from Stirling choosing his teams from a nationalistic POV, going with only English teams after leaving Maserati. His strategy worked for 1958, when he and Tony Brooks took Vanwall to the very first Constructors Championship, but Stirling missed the drivers' title by that one heart-breaking point. And the following years Stirling drove for private entrant Rob Walker, who made a heroic effort but was substantially hampered by the lack of any factory funding. Still that was to Stirling's liking because—and this is part of the Moss Creed—an easy win is a forgettable win. Unearned. Only a hard win is *deserved,* and when you're underfunded, every victory is a hard one.

On the brighter side of the record book, Stirling took more FI pole positions than Jack Brabham in the year of Jack's world title. He gave Lotus its first grande epreuve win, at Monaco 1960, in such rain that only four cars were actually running at the end (Moss, McLaren, Phil Hill and Tony Brooks). Also in 1960, he broke a variety of bones in a crash at Spa, missed three of the nine races, recovered in seven weeks, and finished third in the standings. He earned podium finishes in over one-third of the races he entered. He *won* nearly one out of every four of his races.

Of the long-distance events, he famously won the Mille Miglia with Denis Jenkinson in 1955, beating Fangio by half an hour. He did an astounding three-peat at the Nurburgring 1000 km (620 miles), winning in 1958 and 1959 in an Aston Martin, and in 1960 sharing a Maserati with Dan Gurney. (For comparison, no driver has ever won the Indy 500 more than twice in a row.)

He survived a long stretch of some of Formula One's deadliest seasons—and loved nearly every minute of it. Racing offered something he could get his teeth into. During one of our conversations he said, "Motor racing to me, and I think to many who take part in it, is the greatest challenge the world can offer because the stakes are so high."

To the comment that racing is a lot safer these days, he agreed but said, "You can't make motor racing *safe,* and the only way to make it safe is to stop people racing, really." As he explained to Maurice Hamilton in an interview for *FI Racing* magazine for January 2013, p. 110, "I like playing with fire . . . The fact that there is danger on your shoulder certainly sharpens up your attitude towards what you are doing."

"When you get killed," Stirling told me, "you step off the boat." His overall viewpoint is that all the safety measures are fine in that drivers these days rarely get killed racing. His caveat is that those measures give a driver a sense of security that is dangerously false.

After his '62 accident, he described to me his attempt to return to FI. "My reflexes were all right," he said, "but they were conscious. I knew exactly what to do, but I had to wait til I got the message to do it, whereas before the accident I would do a thing automatically because it was my sixth sense to do it."

For Stirling, racing was far more personalized back in the day. Drivers were visible, for one thing; their heads stuck up above everything else on the car; you could see them check their mirrors (or not), lean against the g-forces, grimace with effort. They also showed their humanity during a race by gesturing, yelling, swearing, waving, blowing kisses to fans, hammering the side of the car, etc.

Today, the driver has become only one piece of a vast technological effort. What do FI fans see? A helmet, sunk deep in the trough of a cockpit. It could be that only through a movie like *Senna* or *I* or *Rush* will a fan get a feel for the man, the human creature, who's out there flashing by at 200 mph.

What did Stirling do with himself after his premature retirement? He starred in marketing pieces for many products and businesses. He appeared at car shows. He raced in VIP events. He competed in historic car festivals. Until just recently, he drove in demanding rally events around the world. He buys and redevelops old London properties.

Since at least the early 1960s, he's lived in the same house—a place that was bombed out during WW II, which he bought and rebuilt to his own design in 1962. Its four stories are filled with the latest gadgets, many of which he himself has invented or designed (he's an FIE, a Fellow of the Institute of Engineers). As much as possible is automatic. He's never moved, maybe because whenever he wants to improve his living situation, he has the skills and energy to simply remodel.

He and his third wife, Lady Susie, married in 1980. When his daughter Allison (by his second wife) was eight years old, she was racing 35 mph small-scale cars. Recently, she climbed to the summit of Mount Kilimanjaro—a Moss, through and through.

Aside from the Queen, it could be said that no other living English public figure has so endured globally and has such high name recognition as . . . Sir Stirling Moss. (Keep in mind that James Bond is fictional, and that Jackie Stewart and Sean Connery are Scots, that Elton John came later, and how many folks under 50 can name the two surviving Beatles?)

What makes him so legendary? Is it his fighting against all odds, driving for an independent team that took on the big factory teams—and so often winning? Or his very early awareness of marketability? His practice of keeping a high profile? His exuberant energy? Unearthly skills? All of those, and more. The very fact that he was arguably the best driver of his time (Stirling would add, "after Fangio retired") yet never won the World Driving Championship puts him in a class by himself. And there he stays. Unique. Compelling. Sought-after and nearly universally recognized more than fifty years after he retired.

In March 2010, he started to board the elevator in his four-story home—only the car wasn't there. He plunged two stories down the shaft, smashing both legs from knees to toes. He'd recovered from so many racing injuries during his long career that he claims this was just another rehab. But this time the after-effects lingered and forced him to slow down a bit.

On January 19, 2018, he announced his retirement from public life. He's moved into a more private phase of his life, but he's left behind a shimmering legacy that will never dim.

Stirling holds forth at The Glen, 1969. He won the USGP once, in 1960 at the Riverside, California track in Rob Walker's private-entry Lotus.

Stirling relaxes with the author in 1970. His conversations range far and wide, at the maximum speed of human speech, and reflect his insatiable curiosity and broad knowledge.

Backed by a California ice plant hillside, the author's husband, Rodger, gets some terracing tips from Stirling in 1970.

Always hatching projects and conducting business at every opportunity, Stirling chats with a contact at the 1971 Laguna Seca Can-Am race eventually won by Peter Revson's McLaren.

JACKIE OLIVER
England August 14, 1942

Jackie Oliver endured plain bad luck for years in F1, driving cars that broke down, for teams often on the skids. Not averse to speaking his mind, he blamed the big teams, especially Ferrari, for always changing the rules whenever smaller teams seemed to be gaining on 'em.

When things were going to hell in a bucket, Jabby Crombac, the eminent Swiss F1 journalist-cum-publisher and early Oliver supporter, got Jackie a NASCAR ride. For one whole season, Jackie experienced the full frontal stock-car culture before high-tailing it back into F1. Back on familiar ground, he still never won a grand prix, and he earned just a handful of championship points over many seasons.

What Jackie did do, however, was make his mark as an endurance driver. With, for example, Pedro Rodriguez (like) and Jacky Ickx (not so much), he won the Le Mans 24 Hour and the Daytona 24 Hour and the Monza 1000 km. He also earned the 1974 Can-Am championship in a Shadow-Chevrolet that was, if I remember correctly, a dark maroon like his helmet.

After he shelved his driving gloves, his luck as a team owner pretty much matched his luck as a grand prix driver. Full of plans and always on the move, he was one of the founders and for many years the owner of the ill-fated Arrows F1 team that was begun in 1977. Over the next 21 years and through hundreds of grands prix, the Arrows team won not a single race. The team was sold, bought back, sold again, going through several iterations that led nowhere.

One could say that the team's single achievement was to eventually give Oliver a secure financial future—finally putting to rest a hefty chunk of his bad luck.

Two congenial drivers enjoy the March sun at the Questor GP. Jackie wasn't entered, but endurance ace Jo Siffert, left, drove his BRM to 6th.

Jackie and his Shadow would win the Can-Am Championship in 1974, the final year for the big thundercars. Here at Laguna Seca in 1971, however, he retired early.

JOSÉ CARLOS PACE
Brazil (October 6, 1944 - March 18, 1977, Age 32)

"Moco" cut his teeth in the same racing milieu as Emerson and Wilson Fittipaldi, and he rode the Brazilian racing wave right to the same top, Formula 1. From local karting races to Formula 3 to Formula 2, he worked his way onto the Williams F1 team for 1972 and Surtees for 1973. Along the way, he hopped into Scuderia Ferrari sports cars for endurance races, with his best finish a second at the '73 Le Mans, co-driving with Arturo Merzario.

He and team owner John Surtees didn't always see eye-to-eye, so for 1974 Moco joined Bernie Ecclestone's Brabham team. Few achievements for a driver are rarer or more emotional than winning one's home F1 race, and Pace did exactly that at the Brazilian Interlagos circuit in São Paulo in 1975; tens of thousands of Brazilian fans madly celebrated the one-two finish of not only Moco but his countryman-hero, Emmo Fittipaldi (both far ahead of Graham Hill in his final championship grand prix). That same year, Moco and teammate Carlos Reutemann boosted the Brabham-Ford to second place in the Constructors Championship.

The next year was a struggle, but things were looking up for the '77 season. Between the deadly South African GP on March 5 and the USGP West in April at Long Beach, Moco returned home to São Paulo for a brief holiday. After visiting an old friend's farm, he and his friend were nearly back in the city when their light plane went down, killing them both.

The Interlagos circuit was renamed Autodromo José Carlos Pace in his honor and, except for the 1980s, has hosted the Brazilian Grand Prix every year since.

Moco helped start a line of future Brazilian drivers that would include three World Champions: Emerson Fittipaldi, Nelson Piquet and Ayrton Senna. Here at the 1972 USGP, he consults with Ron Tauranac, who would shortly sell his Brabham team to Bernie Ecclestone.

HENRI PESCAROLO
France September 25, 1942

What an adventurer! It's hard to know what to emphasize with Henri, so take your pick:

- his seven seasons in lethal Formula 1;
- his status as a Le Mans legend, having entered the exhausting race 33 times—a record, 30 of them consecutively, also a record—the last when he was 57 years old;
- his long and successful record in endurance racing;
- his eight entries in the hair-raising Dakar Rally;
- his jaunts as a helicopter pilot;
- his 1984 record for the fastest flight across the Atlantic in a single-engine plane, with Patrick Fourticq;
- his stints as a movie stunt driver;
- his Pescarolo Sport team that fielded sports cars from 2005 until closing in 2013.

In F1, he drove for four teams and entered dozens of grands prix, but his greatest triumphs came in the long-distance events. For obvious reasons, he favored the French Matra and Ligier race cars. Wearing his apple-green helmet, he amassed four Le Mans victories (three of them consecutive, like Stirling Moss) and finished best in class an additional two times.

The last few years, however, have seen disaster strike this Frenchman who considers himself lucky to be alive. Racing crashes, testing accidents, bankruptcy, ill health have all piled on to wallop him severely. Recoveries have been slow, but they *are* recoveries, and Henri carries on, no doubt drawing on the same spirit and strength that made him an adventurer in the first place.

Always on his way to somewhere, Henri gets a quiet walk through the Ontario, California circuit byways at the 1971 Questor GP.

Henri confers with his crew at the Questor GP at the wheel of his March, the team named by and for Mosley (Max), Alan Reese, Coaker (Graham) and Herd (Robin).

Henri feels no need for a parka at a frigid Watkins Glen, 1972. He would push his March seven places higher than where he started.

RONNIE PETERSON
Sweden (February 14, 1944 - September 11, 1978, Age 34)

Ronnie was fast, and he was sure. He shot to the top smoothly, moving from karting to F3 to F1. In his first F1 race, driving an independent March-Ford at the 1970 Monaco GP, he finished seventh. His first year in a factory-team March-Ford, 1971, he finished the season second only to that year's World Champion, Jackie Stewart. His first year with Lotus-Ford, 1973, he won four of the 15 championship races. Surely he would win a championship in no time at all!

The Formula One gods don't work that way, however. His next next two years with unsuccessful Lotus cars were frustrating, so 1976 saw him back at March, where he was plagued by retirements except for his single victory at Monza. And after a slow year with Tyrrell, he returned to Lotus for 1978 as teammate to Mario Andretti. The two of them dominated the championship to such an extent that the only question was, which one would win the title?

Andretti won the Argentine, Belgian, Spanish, French, German, and Dutch GPs; he finished second at Long Beach in the USGP West. But all those wins didn't mean the championship was virtually his, because Ronnie Peterson was piling up points by placing second in Belgium, Spain, France and the Netherlands, plus outright winning in South Africa and Austria.

With three races left, Mario had 63 points and Ronnie had 51. Both knew that the dozen-points difference could be erased by highly likely combinations of Peterson wins and/or high placings, with Andretti very apt to retire as he had in five races already. Third and fourth in the standings were Niki Lauda and Carlos Reutemann, both roughly 30 points behind Mario but poised to mathematically poach on Peterson's second place. The final trio of grands prix looked to be cliff-hangers.

That was the setting for the Italian GP at Monza, which never needs added suspense. It is still very very fast and in 1978 the configuration, especially around the start/finish segment, promised built-in trouble.

This one race held nearly all the mistakes, bad luck, terror and injuries that were normally spread out over several events. The whole race—beginning, middle, end, and aftermath—was so bizarre, horrendous and tragic that describing the main points might give readers a fair idea of what FI people and drivers risked (and still do, although today's cars and tracks are far safer).

Ronnie Peterson had won the Italian GP a whopping three times in eight years ('73, '74 and '76). In 1978, everything that could go wrong in one race, did so at Monza. It started when Peterson demolished his Lotus-Ford in practice. The back-up car was unfit to race, so the tall Peterson uncomfortably squashed into the spare car fitted to the smaller Mario Andretti.

The start-finish area and grid were 50 yards wide. Within two seconds at FI starting speeds, the track narrowed to 15 yards, just before the first curve. Now add a clumsy signal by the flagman-starter, which got the middle rows going before the front rows, which further bunched the grid as they charged into that first curve.

Various re-tellings accuse/defend various drivers as having started the crash that ensued and wrecked ten cars in the first three seconds. The upshot was that Ronnie got slammed into the Armco barrier. His car burst into flames and hurtled back onto the track. James Hunt, Patrick Depailler and Clay Regazzoni rushed to Ronnie's burning car and heroically pulled him out. Arturo Merzario, Didier Pironi and other racers helped rescue a second driver, Vittorio Brambilla, who appeared more gravely injured (but would recover to race again).

Ronnie's legs were so obviously mangled that Hunt diverted Peterson from seeing them. In addition, Ronnie suffered minor burns and had inhaled gasoline fumes. Although the melee had taken place just 800 yards from the starting grid, 17 agonizing minutes passed before Ronnie got loaded into an ambulance.

It took nearly three hours to clean up the track, whereupon two drivers jumped the re-start, resulting in penalties that juggled the finishing order.

Meanwhile at the hospital, Ronnie's one leg was broken in seven places, the other in three. He underwent surgery that night and appeared to be stabilized. But fatal damage had already been inflicted by an unseen bone marrow embolism traveling through his bloodstream to vital organs. Near dawn he slipped into a coma and he died mid-morning, before his wife could reach his bedside.

More fallout from that race included Ronnie's widow and toddler left behind, poisonous recriminations within the GPDA, a criminal trial, an eventual suicide, an orphan, a redesigned track at Monza, and a museum that opened and folded within 16 months. Various websites contain the bleak details.

The 1978 season closed with Mario Andretti becoming the second American to earn the World Championship. Carlos Reutemann and his Ferrari tried valiantly to gain 2nd place, but came up just three points short of Ronnie's total. Niki Lauda in a Brabham-Alfa Romeo finished in 4th. Lotus took the Constructors title by a huge margin over Ferrari, thanks to Mario and Ronnie.

Ronnie Peterson had streaked onto the F1 scene, and when he had a car up to his superb capabilities, he was all but unbeatable. His first full year and his last were his best. He was surely headed for multiple championships, probably in multiple marques. It's unusual for a driver to return to a team he once left. It's unusual for a team to take back a driver they once parted with. Ronnie left March and returned, and he left Lotus and returned. That speaks tetrabytes for his adjustable and harmonious personality.

That also figures into why he's remembered as the "Super Swede."

Destined to finish 2nd to Jackie Stewart in the 1971 driving championship, Ronnie and his March started that year slowly, finishing 18th here at the Questor GP.

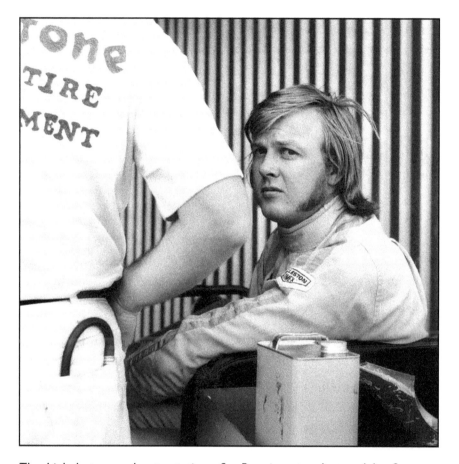

The high hopes and expectations for Ronnie got sabotaged by frequent retirements, great teams at their low points, and, finally, a brilliant talent snuffed out.

SAM POSEY
United States May 26, 1944

Sam Posey designed a firehouse. And a school. And 45 homes. And furniture. He's written two books, *The Mudge Pond Express* (G.P. Putnam, 1975) and *Playing With Trains* (Random House, 2004). Rhode Island School of Design alumnus. Sportswriter, general writer, essayist, Emmy winner, TV commentator, and did I mention professional artist?

Why in the world did this man, who could've chosen to focus on so many safer things, choose to pilot a race car? In what he himself described as "the deadliest sport in the world"? Simply put, until one very specific day and time, he was in it to win it. More articulate than most of us, Sam waxed rapturous in a 1969 article for the *New York Times:* "I race cars . . . [for] the sheer joy of hurling a 200 mph racing car through a steep downhill turn—the world passing in a blur, the car at the very limit of adhesion."

Sam experienced that joy in sports cars first, then Trans Am and USAC Champ cars. He added the monster Can-Am cars and the Indy 500. Ten times over a dozen years, he entered Le Mans, doing his best with a third place in 1971[5] driving a Ferrari with fellow Yankee Tony Adamowicz. He won the 1971 Sebring 12 Hours co-driving a BMW with Hans-Joachim Stuck, Brian Redman and Allan Moffat. He raced a Surtees-Chevrolet in the '71 and '72 USGPs at Watkins Glen.

But it was on June 20, 1976, that Sam realized the grim reality of racing open-wheel, open-cockpit cars. He'd carried on despite the death of one friend each year for three prior years—each one on the track, each one because of a sudden mechanical failure.[6] He himself

---

5   The 1971 Le Mans 24 Hour was won by Helmut Marko and Gijs van Lennep. Yes, <u>that</u> Helmut Marko, the Dr. Marko who today advises and does driver development for the Red Bull F1 team in another illustration of how interwoven the small world of F1 is. Much is forgiven, but very little is ever forgotten, and everything comes full circle, often in unexpected ways.

6   Swede Savage 1973. Peter Revson 1974. Mark Donohue 1975.

had survived a couple of terrible, avert-your-eyes crashes. But that day in June at an F5000 race at Mosport, Canada, while sitting on the grid waiting for the starting signal—heart pumping, nerves strung tight—with no warning Sam flashed on the brutal reality that he, too, could and probably would get snuffed out in a race car.

Immediately after that race, he took the only action a die-hard racer could take: He beefed up the odds in his favor. He forsook the open-cockpit cars and concentrated exclusively on full-bodied cars like coupes and sedans.

Meanwhile, he was writing books and newspaper articles, and his columns regularly delighted *Road & Track* readers. As if that weren't enough, he was also easing into TV as a commentator. One could say he was over-qualified, with his years of varied racing experience, his infectious enthusiasm, his compassionate viewpoint, his articulateness. ABC Sports realized their good fortune in signing him, and before long Sam was covering not only the Indy series and NASCAR but the Tour de France and the Winter Olympics. Eventually, he joined the Speed Channel, and when NBC took on Formula One telecasts, Sam continued his enlightening and thoughtful segments of "Posey's Perspective."

One of his mates on the NBC Sports telecast was David Hobbs. Lucky is the fly on the wall when the droll David and the prank-loving Sam got together!

Health issues these days preclude any TV work, and they sharply cut down on the hours he can devote to his artwork, with Parkinson's disease slowing him considerably. Still, he disappears into his studio as often as possible. Not many artists can claim, as Posey can, that his works hang in several prestigious galleries—the Tate in London being just one of them.

Sam embodies the modern Renaissance man. He has left a lasting mark, and so many facets of life including Formula One are richer for his many contributions.

Affable, loquacious, erudite, that's Sam. Here he soaks up the atmosphere of a Can-Am race in 1971 at Laguna Seca.

Driving a Surtees at The Glen in 1972, Sam finished 12th of the 31 entries, just behind Graham Hill's Brabham. His perspective was broad and deep, combining the aesthetics of motor racing with an appreciation of racing history.

BRIAN REDMAN
England March 9, 1937

One of the true gentlemen of Formula One, Brian gave FI a good try now and then but never enjoyed the atmosphere and far preferred endurance events. He revealed much of the reason in a 2010 interview with Richard Jenkins, at www.oldracingcars.com. (Read the entire interview and you'll get a great picture of how some careers were built back in the day.) Brian told Jenkins, " . . . Jackie Stewart, Jody Scheckter, Niki Lauda, they all had that burning desire to excel themselves. Well, I never had that at the same level as them, and so I became happy enjoying and loving what I was doing and that was enough."

Brian's "enough" would make many race drivers ecstatic. He won the squirrelly Targa Florio in 1970 with Jo Siffert in a Porsche. He won the Kyalami 9 Hour in 1971 co-driving a Ferrari with Clay Regazzoni and beating the Ickx/Andretti Ferrari by 15 laps. He won the Spa 1000 km in 1972 sharing a team Ferrari with Arturo Merzario. He drove with the best and against the best, and he joined the ranks of being the best. He built a superb reputation and a shining legacy in endurance racing.

As for the American F5000 series, Brian drove a Jim Hall/Carl Haas Lola to the championship title not once, not twice, but three times, in '74, '75 and '76.

I suggest that he turned out to have as much grit and "burning desire" as any driver. How else to explain his several serious injuries, followed by grinding recoveries, followed by popping up again on the grid at the next possible race? For example, at the Mont Tremblant F5000 race in 1977, he completely smashed his entire left side from neck to foot. But who showed up at the 1978 Sebring 12 Hour event—*and won it?* Right, and he was 40 years old. If that isn't a man excelling himself, we need new definitions.

For all his guts and glory, Brian is a very gracious man, a very kind person. He has a wonderful sense of humor and more patience than most. He's still involved in racing through a marketing firm, vintage cars, driving schools and *Road & Track*. In 2018, he brought out his autobiography, *Brian Redman: Daring Drivers, Deadly Tracks*.

If you happen to attend one of the many historic car events, especially around Florida where Brian and his family live, give special attention to a white-haired, curly-headed driver with a broad English accent. Once one of the fastest men on earth, he's still one of the nicest.

At the height of the McLaren domination of the Can-Am series, Brian would bring his BRM home in 4th at the 1971 Laguna Seca event.

Brian strategizes with his Team Manager, Tim Parnell, at The Glen, 1972. Despite their best efforts, the car had other ideas and Brian DNFd.

CLAY REGAZZONI
Switzerland (September 5, 1939 - December 15, 2006, Age 67)

Clay was a highly popular driver, no matter where or when. Dedicated and driven, still he had a relaxed persona as he made his way through F2, F1, the podium, the DNF list, in racing, on TV, at public appearances. He radiated a palpable presence and was always ready to break into a big warm smile.

He raced for his team owner, for his team, and for his own joy, in that order. Money played but a small part in his scheme of things. In this he may have been a step behind his colleagues and the sport of F1, which in the 1970s was growing more and more commercial at a remarkable clip.

Clay is another rare example (like Ronnie Peterson) of a driver returning to a former team, and he did it twice. He was welcomed back into, of all teams, Ferrari after a year away with BRM; and later, he returned to the Ensign team he'd driven for earlier.

It's arguably every driver's secret wish to drive for Ferrari. Clay sat in that catbird seat through 1970, '71 and '72 and again for '74, '75 and '76. The *tifosi* loved him, and at Monza where he won twice, they adored him more than ever. In the end, however, Ferrari treated him like any of its drivers—that is to say, not well. Not given to sulking, Clay happily spent the next season with the small Ensign team, then '78 with Shadow and the next year with Williams.

Clay created a historic event at the 1979 British GP at Silverstone when he earned Frank Williams his marque's very first F1 victory after ten years of struggle. The Williams team these days has well over 700 grands prix in the record books, but Frank will never forget that first win or that it was Clay Regazzoni who achieved it.

For the 1980 season, Clay rejoined Ensign. He was driving an Ensign-Ford at the USGP West at Long Beach when his life took a violent turn. His braking failed and he slammed into a concrete barrier, snapping his spine and leaving him a paraplegic.

Five very dark years followed—years of desperation, agony, effort, and adjusting to all aspects of his changed life. A resilient Clay emerged to become a positive force for improving the equipment available to disabled motorists. He became a TV race commentator. He began driving in rallies in cars with hand controls. He started a driving school for the disabled. At what cost we'll never know, but he became the New Clay, as modest, respected and loved as the Old Clay. Only someone in that same spot can grasp what it must've taken to carve out a new life, then to even *want* to return to racing—any racing—and *then* to get himself in shape for those grueling events *and* learn to drive hand-controlled cars under race conditions. He didn't stop racing such sports cars until he was 62—and then only because the FIA didn't renew his license.

A formula racing driver of his era could expect to die in his car. So very many did. But Clay would die driving a passenger car, on an everyday Italian road, in the middle of winter, just outside Parma. That dark December day, he joined other FI drivers Nino Farina, Mike Hawthorn, and Mike Hailwood as a traffic fatality.

His funeral in Lugano, attended by many of the FI drivers he'd competed against, was two days before Christmas.

In F1 there's always activity and there's always hurry-up-and-wait—usually simultaneously. Clay's Ferrari gets an adjustment under Giorgio Tavoni's supervision prior to the 1972 USGP. In a bit of symmetry, Clay's #8 took 8th place in the race.

In this all-Ferrari ballet at The Glen in 1972, Clay leads Andretti and Ickx. They would finish in the exact opposite order: Jacky 5th, Mario 6th and Clay 8th.

CARLOS REUTEMANN
Argentina April 12, 1942

As a Southern Hemisphere autumn descended upon Argentina in 1942, a baby boy was born into a cattleman's family. Who would've guessed that the little one would someday command his entire province from the governor's desk? Or that he'd figuratively drive to that governorship in an F1 race car?

The path to political eminence was unprecedented, unforeseen, unplanned and certainly refreshing for all involved. While it's true that politics plays a huge role in Formula 1, the skills learned there don't usually translate into the entirely different realm of *political* politics. Unless you're Carlos Reutemann.

Not since the great Juan Manuel Fangio had Argentina offered the world an F1 contender. Fangio retired in 1958, and it was a long dozen years before Reutemann made his European F2 appearance. He'd done touring and formula racing back home convincingly enough that the Automobile Club of Argentina sponsored the 28-year old as he broke into the international scene. In only his second season in the new environment of European racing, he beat out every other F2 driver save one, when Ronnie Peterson won the series title.

This drew the sharp eye of the Brabham team's new owner, Bernie Ecclestone, who signed Carlos to the F1 team for 1972. Reutemann's very first F1 race was his home grand prix of Argentina. Hopes ran high for "Lole's" success. The racing gods smiled upon him as he went out and, to the astonishment of some and the glee of others, grabbed the pole. In his first-ever Formula One race! In a car he hadn't even raced yet! Argentine fans went crazy. Their hopes and his, however, faltered along with the car, and he finished in seventh, just out of the points.

He was an excellent qualifier who then proved himself in the crucible and chaos of competition: In 31% of the nearly 150 grands prix he entered, he ended up on the podium as one of the top three finishers—an amazing record.

With his dark, hooded eyes, his mane of dark hair and square jaw, he projected a fierce, brooding look. That was accompanied by an aura of quiet, measured confidence. But whatever emotions were busy inside, he kept to himself.

After three years with the Brabham team, he moved to Ferrari for two seasons, then Lotus for one. He joined the Williams team in 1980, and in 1981 came *this* close—one point, a fourth gear and an increasingly oversteering car—to winning the World Championship.

Politics giveth and politics taketh away. That may have been the case with Carlos, who was driving for an English team during the British-Argentine/Falklands-Malvinas War in April 1982. Whatever—if anything—occurred between Carlos and the Williams team, Reutemann's F1 career ended abruptly. Immediately after the Brazilian GP in March he left the team and returned to his home in Santa Fe.

He was 40 years old with a wife and a family and no job. In an unexpected and creative move, he edged into local politics. In fewer than nine years, the over three million citizens of his Santa Fe province elected him governor. He served his first four-year term from 1991 to 1995. Argentine law mandated that he then take at least one term off. As soon as it was legal, he ran again and was elected to his second stint from 1999 to 2003.

Unluckily for him but luckily for Santa Fe, he was in charge when Argentina was hit with the economic crash of 2001. Thanks to his fiscally wise policies, his province weathered the scary period far better than most provinces. He then found his party begging him to run for president of Argentina. How many folks, let alone F1 drivers, have *that* on their résumé?

Following his own gyroscope, Carlos declined—but he did consent to run for one of Santa Fe's three National Senate seats and in 2003 won that election. His home province wanted him back as governor in 2007, but again he declined the offer, preferring to be effective as

Senator Reutemann.

A year earlier, on January 1, 2006, the President of Italy, Carlo Ciampi, made Carlos a *Commendatore della Repubblica.* Like Mario Andretti, Carlos may now and forever be addressed as Commendatore Reutemann.

In 2009 he won re-election to Argentina's National Senate for another six-year term, and when that was up in 2015, his strong Santa Fe support sent him right back. Throughout his senatorial service, he has played a big part in what turned out to be his country's fifteen-year struggle with debt restructuring, caused by that deep four-year recession at the start of the Millennium. He fights for his province so effectively that if his health permits and if he wants it, his constituents will no doubt again confirm him as their Senator when elections roll around in 2021.

A man of many esteemed titles—Commendatore, Governor, Senator–Carlos remains a very active supporter of motor racing. It wouldn't surprise me if he's involved in the current efforts to bring F1 back to Argentina with an Argentine Grand Prix in Buenos Aires. And Carlos would like nothing better than to send some promising new Argentine driver into F1.

If and when that young man/woman comes along, s/he has some mighty big shoes to fill.

Gazing far ahead at the 1972 USGP, Carlos could not have foreseen that someday he would wield profound political clout in his beloved Argentina.

Any first corner of any race holds peril for all, and at The Glen in 1972, Carlos got smacked, guaranteeing that he would eventually retire his Brabham.

PETER REVSON
United States (February 27, 1939 - March 22, 1974, Age 35)

Finally, an American F1 driver who was a contender for the world championship! Not since Dan Gurney had Americans had sustained cause to cheer. Then along came Peter.

Outsiders labeled Peter Revson a wealthy playboy, a millionaire jet-setter who dabbled in fast cars and fast living. To insiders like his teammates and the racing press, though, he ranked among the top for dedication and talent and seriousness of purpose.

When he was 23, he and Cornell classmate Timmy Mayer formed a Formula Junior team and picked Tim's older brother Teddy to manage it. They raced in Europe and elsewhere for the 1963-64 season, until Timmy was killed in a 1964 Tasman Series race.

Peter then formed Revson Racing managed by Reg Parnell, but they gained little except experience in a Lotus-BRM. So Peter raced the big Group 7 Can-Am cars from 1966-1970.

His younger brother Doug died in a formula car race in Denmark in 1967, but Peter pressed on. In his autobiography, *Speed With Style*, written with *Autoweek* publisher at the time Leon Mandel, Peter said, "The thought of being killed does occur to you if you're a racing driver. But if it occurred a lot, you couldn't drive." In another quote from his autobiography, he said, "I know if I make any mistakes . . . I'm going to lose. And that's as bad as anything I can visualize. . . Losing really hurts. To fail in the race is the most painful thing imaginable."

His driving style was smooth, fast and conservative, whether in F1, Can-Am, Trans-Am or Indy cars. He was known to nurse faltering cars to the finish when other drivers would have parked and walked away.

In 1969, Peter was runner-up rookie of the year to Mark Donohue at the Indy 500; 1970 saw him co-drive the Sebring 12 Hours with Steve McQueen; he was Donohue's teammate on the Penske Trans

Am team; in 1971 he won the Can-Am championship *and* took the pole at the Indy 500 where he finished second.

All this made him a prime candidate for Formula One, so in 1972 he went with the McLaren F1 team managed by Teddy Mayer. (You'll notice that the same names and the same families keep popping up in different combinations, illustrating once again the very small world of F1.)

In only his second year with a first-class outfit, Peter won two grands prix–the British and the Canadian. He won them in a Yardley McLaren-Ford. This raised a stink with Uncle Charles, who ran the family Revlon cosmetics empire. Yardley! A direct competitor to Revlon! Horrors! However, Peter much earlier had asked for Revlon sponsorship and the family had turned him down. Not one to gloat over his Yardley victories, Peter reportedly simply shrugged off the awkward situation.

He was on a roll and he knew it. But during the 1973 silly season, the 34-year old felt the hot breath of youth on his neck as McLaren leaned toward letting Peter go and taking on the 23-year-old Jody Scheckter instead. Peter may have been on a roll, but rumor had it that McLaren didn't see it that way. The Associated Press quoted Peter as saying, "I feel the way Hank Aaron would if the Braves were to let him go the season after he breaks Babe Ruth's home run record."

Was the rumor true, was he signing with a different team for 1974? Up and down the pits the word was: Shadow. So at a Shadow team party, several of us racing writers approached Peter with hearty congratulations. He grinned with exaggerated innocence, saying, "Did I have a baby or something?" We brought his signing out in the open, and then he cheerily discussed it without hesitation.

Often described as a free spirit, he was easy to talk with, funny, upbeat. Through no apparent effort on his part, his warm friendliness instantly won over even jaded folks. He could be direct and honest with the press without being confessional or brutal about it. He was one of the best-liked drivers in the business, from mogul to gofer to motorsports press.

Outside Johannesburg, South Africa, lies the Kyalami racing circuit. Back in the day, it was one of the fastest tracks in FI. Drivers loved lolling by the hotel pool in the warm African sun when it was cold and rainy in Europe, but many of them felt that the circuit itself was more dangerous than need be. In preparation for the 1974 race there, several teams arrived ten or so days ahead of the race to do some testing. The Shadow team was one such, with their new driver Peter Revson.

When you're in the pits and cars are out on the track, whether during testing or practice or qualifying or the race, your mind incorporates the steady scream of engines out on the circuit. When one howling suddenly stops, heads fly up, hearts clench, bodies meerkat to hear announcements and see up the track. Peter's front suspension broke and he exploded into the Armco barrier along what was called Barbeque Bend. Other drivers were circulating at the same time, and Graham Hill and Denny Hulme instantly braked, leaped out, and ran to Peter's flaming car. Risking injuries themselves, they pulled Peter out and tried to save him. It was heroism in ghastly circumstances that sear the memory, the worse for having failed.

Why did still another driver have to die before common-sense safety measures were implemented? Immediately after Peter's death, the solid barrier he crashed into was replaced with triple catch fencing in time for the race.

Two days before the race, hundreds attended Peter's funeral in Manhattan. Roger Penske and Mandel offered eulogies. Then Peter was taken to rest beside his brother Doug in the family crypt in Westchester County, New York.

Peter had clinched the Can-Am championship before the 1971 Laguna Seca race, so he could have stroked his way through. Instead, he tore off and won it like the true racer he was.

Despite his privileged upbringing and all the perks that go with it, Peter's obvious talent and hard work earned him the whole-hearted respect of his FI colleagues—folks who are not easily impressed.

JOCHEN RINDT

Austrian (April 18, 1942 - September 5, 1970, Age 28)

Jochen Rindt was a diamond in the rough. He acquired polish as he went along, but he essentially remained blunt and unchanged to the end.

Hot-tempered. Sensitive. Anti-authoritarian. Cooperative. Prankish. Serious. A ruffian. A sophisticate. Jochen was all of those and more. He joined declining teams at exactly the wrong times, and just when he was finding his footing and lady luck was starting to shine on him, it all ended.

It began the same way it was to end: tragically. In late July of 1943, his Austrian mother and German father were killed in "Operation Gomorrah," the historic Allied bombing of Hamburg, Germany, in WW II. Over three days, 30,000 of the city's 230,000 people were killed—among them, Jochen's family. Fifteen-month-old Jochen somehow survived and was taken in by his mother's parents, a lawyer and his wife, at their home in Graz, Austria. His grandparents raised him there, and there is conflicting info about whether Jochen ever officially became an Austrian citizen; he may technically have been German, although he forever raced as an Austrian, for Austria.

Competitive sports consumed his young years, when he became a crack tennis player and excellent skier (although he broke his leg twice on the slopes). His grandfather was a very modern-thinking man who let Jochen explore and experience nearly everything he wanted to. Not included in Jochen's field of interest were school and anyone in authority. He and his Graz buddies gleefully thumbed their noses at rules and restrictions and those who would try to enforce them. Luckily for Jochen, his grandfather was highly respected and well-connected and could smooth things over with the local authorities.

Among Jochen's pals was a boy a year and nine days younger, Helmut Marko, whose near future looked to keep pace with Jochen's. The racing bug bit both of them early and often but there were no local races, so the boys staged their own. Before they and their friends were old enough to get drivers' licenses, they raced mopeds up and down the quiet streets of Graz. A moped's top speed was supposedly 50 mph, but Jochen could push his up to 70.

Life's highs and lows were compacted into his next three years. His Grandfather Martinowitz died; his grandmother bought him an Alfa that he raced. Then his grandmother died, and with his inheritance he bought a used Formula Junior Cooper. By his 21st birthday his family was gone and he was all on his own. But he had a direction: Become a full-time racing driver. As Jochen took off toward that goal, his pal Helmut Marko took off for law school in Vienna and an eventual doctorate.

During Jochen's early F3 races, he met the daughter of a famous driver from Finland, Curt Lincoln. Nina and Jochen continued their friendship on the ski slopes as well as race tracks. He was entering more and better races, quickly catching the attention of people of importance in motor racing. Support and major races followed. At age 22 he found himself on the grid of the Austrian Grand Prix, where he joined 11 of the 20 starters in the DNF column, having retired Rob Walker's Brabham-BRM halfway through because of mechanical failure. His speed and intensity weren't overlooked, however, and John Cooper signed him to his F1 team for 1965.

On June 20th of that year, Rindt and Masten Gregory pulled off a stunning, impossible victory at the Le Mans 24 Hour race by driving an older Ferrari that American Ferrari dealer Luigi Chinetti entered against all the factory teams. Little did Jochen know that was to be the highlight of his year. Jim Clark cleaned up nearly every grand prix victory (except for Monza, where a youngster named Jackie Stewart won), and for Jochen it was a learning year. His driving was labeled "wild," not without some basis. But it was also precise and extremely fast, and except for that first 1965, in every year after that if Jochen finished a race, he finished in the points, in the top six. It was all or nothing, either points or retired. As John Surtees told me about

Jochen's early FI driving, "Oh at times, probably, he was rather zestful or lacking in experience . . . but this applies to a lot of people when they're starting. You can't know it all immediately, and if you've got the will and the 'go' in you, well, you probably take risks in ignorance to some extent, and get out of the situations often by having a natural ability."

Reflecting on Jochen's two years with Cooper, his friend Marko later said to me, "He was very unhappy for a couple of seasons for it was more than assured that he and Stewart are the quickest guys around, and he just got bad luck all the time. . . It was some depression on him for he couldn't show his real speed for always something went wrong with the [cars]."

The year 1967 wasn't a total downer, though, because he married his Nina, the beautiful Finnish model. He'd also acquired a savvy young manager named Bernie Ecclestone.

For 1968, Jochen joined the Brabham team, and he and Jack grew very close. He also entered the Indy 500 in 1967 and 1968, but had neither luck nor fun there. In 1968, he also became a father, of Natascha (who would grow up to be tall and look like her dad). He would've liked to have stayed with Brabham, but enter Colin Chapman, who waved so big an offer that Jack couldn't match it and Jochen could not, in all sanity refuse it. Marko explained that by this time Jochen " . . . found very soon what money he can earn and what money's worth, and he was very hot on the money side, and he learned it very quick . . . He knew what value he had." Still, "He wasn't a man who enjoyed life very much," said Marko. "It was sometimes easy to hurt him, but he would never show this . . . Generally, he was a very clear character, with no complexes."

As I learned from watching Jochen in the pits and paddock, he was either joking around or dead serious; I rarely saw anything in between. As for his sense of humor, Marko remarked that Jochen played practical jokes quite often, "but they are all so typical Austrian, I just can't translate it into English." Which is probably just as well . . .

Lotus and Rindt turned out to be a formidable alignment. Lotus got a young driver with enormous talent and promise, and Jochen finally got a car worthy of his skills and style. By the end of 1969, Rindt shot up to fourth in the World Championship and at Watkins Glen climbed the victory platform for the first time.

However, not for the first time, the high price of his profession reared its ugly head as his triumph was dimmed by the devastating injuries that afternoon to his teammate, Graham Hill. Up on the platform, Jochen was for the most part somber at the very moment he should've been jubilant.

He and his Lotus-Ford sailed into 1970 and won five grands prix, starting with every driver's glamor win, Monaco. Then in uninterrupted succession came victories in the Dutch, French, British and German races. He was hugely disappointed to retire in his own Austrian GP, but he knew that with a little luck he was headed for the World Championship. The next race was the Italian at Monza.

During the final practice session, Jochen's Lotus suddenly swerved and shot into the barriers at nearly 200 mph. Death must've been nearly instantaneous, although reports at the time mistakenly hinted that quicker medical attention might have saved him. His friend and manager, Bernie Ecclestone, sprinted to the site and picked up Jochen's bloody helmet and one shoe. When no information was forthcoming from the race officials, close friend Jackie Stewart frantically dashed to the medical center where Jochen lay unattended. Jackie by now knew death when he saw it, and he knew his friend was dead.

Being Italy, there was a court case to fasten blame, and Colin Chapman was charged. Eventually the court found that the safety barriers were badly placed and that Jochen had clipped only four of his five seat belts. That fifth one might have saved his life, but we'll never know. Chapman was exonerated.

Bruce McLaren, June 2, 1970. Piers Courage, June 21, 1970. And now Jochen Rindt, September 5, 1970. Grand prix would close the terrible season with its first posthumous World Champion.

[As a sidebar to Jochen's story, Dr. Helmut Marko would launch his own full-time racing career just months after Jochen's death, when Marko and Gijs van Lennep drove their Porsche to victory in the 1971 Le Mans. Formula One drives followed, until the 1972 French GP when Helmut was hit by a stone shot from the car ahead, costing him an eye and his career. He stayed in racing, running teams in lesser formulae and developing new talent. For several years he's been the liaison between Red Bull chief Dietrich Mateschitz and the F1 team starring first his protégé Sebastian Vettel and then his latest *wunderkind,* Max Verstappen.]

Jochen endured five full seasons without a major win. But here at the 1969 USGP, he's just hours away from his first victory. Once the ice broke, he won five of the next ten and the World Championship (awarded posthumously in a horrendous turn of fate).

Jochen and his boyhood buddy Helmet Marko shared hair-raising escapades in their hometown of Graz, Austria. Maturity did not tame Jochen.

PEDRO RODRIGUEZ
Mexico (January 18, 1940 - July 11, 1971, Age 31)

Pedro was only 13 when he earned his first national motorcycle championship—and 14 when he earned his second. He was a prodigy but an untamed one, so at age 15, to acquire some discipline, he found himself up in the U.S. in a military school. But he'd already attracted the motorsports attention of that great talent-spotter, Luigi Chinetti, the American Ferrari dealer who worked closely with Enzo Ferrari and the Maranello factory.

So it was that at the tender age of 17, Pedro entered his first big-time international race, the Nassau Trophy event, driving a Ferrari for Chinetti's North American Racing Team (NART). Pedro and Chinetti formed an alliance that would last Pedro's lifetime. From then on, all the major endurance races—Le Mans, Sebring, Daytona, the Ring—saw Rodriguez driving NART Ferraris to frequent podium finishes.

Endurance racing, in fact, was where Pedro would make his reputation as a premier driver. The icing on that cake was the fact that he also developed into a rainmaster, turning in top finishes in drizzles and downpours.

Of only six FI drivers from Mexico over the past half century and counting[7], one third of them were from the same family, for Pedro wasn't the only son that the Rodriguez family could cheer on. His younger brother Ricardo had already made a name for himself. He, too, caught Chinetti's eye, and from his early teens raced NART Ferraris. He broke several age records, being the youngest to earn a podium finish at Le Mans, the youngest to start an Italian GP on the front row, and others[8] (see Wikipedia for details on Ricardo).

---

7   Moises Solana, 1963-68, BRM, Lotus; Hector Rebaque, 1977-81, Hesketh, Lotus, Brabham; Esteban Gutierrez, 2013-14 and 2016, Sauber, Haas; and Sergio Perez, 2011-present, Force India/Racing Point.

8   His FI record lasted until the Belgian GP of 2016, when Max Verstappen at 18 years, 332 days became the youngest driver on the front row—only to have *that* record broken by Lance Stroll just a year later at Monza, at 18 years, 329 days.

Three times at Le Mans, the brothers Rodriguez co-drove Ferraris, in 1959, 1961 and 1962; each time the boys were forced to retire with mechanical trouble. At the end of the 1962 season at their home grand prix in Mexico City, the suspension broke on Ricardo's Lotus and the resulting crash killed him instantly. All Mexico mourned his loss, no one more deeply affected than Pedro, who would ever after travel with mementos of his little brother.

Pedro would enter Le Mans 14 times (the record so far is 33 entries by Henri Pescarolo). He won the grueling race once, in 1968, co-driving a John Wyer Ford GT 40 with Lucien Bianchi, great uncle of the future FI driver Jules Bianchi, each Bianchi a racing fatality.

In Formula One, Pedro fluctuated from number two driver to number one, depending on the team. For 1966 with Lotus, he was second to Jim Clark. In 1967 his team leader at Cooper was Jochen Rindt, but Pedro outranked the newcomer Jackie Ickx. On the BRM team for 1968, he took the number one slot of the late Mike Spence. He split 1969 racing a factory Ferrari much of the season and a NART Ferrari in the three North American grands prix: Canada, United States and Mexico. For 1970 and 1971 he played second fiddle to first Peter Revson and then Jackie Oliver on the Yardley BRM Team.

During his nine years in FI, he earned World Championship points in seven of them. But endurance events were where he earned his cabinets full of winner's trophies. Such versatility, though, doesn't come without a price. In 1970, for example, Pedro entered 12 endurance races (won 4 of them) and 13 grand epreuves (won at Spa). That's 25 races in 32 weeks, each event a high-class, high-stress, high-tension, high-risk affair with little rest between any of them. Such was the pressure-cooker life of a top driver even back in those "slower" days.

Different men react to such pressures in different ways. Whenever I ran into Pedro, he was good-natured and open. He moved around in the pits quietly, without flash or fuss. During the long hurry-up-and-wait periods, he'd wear a small smile as he silently observed whatever was going on. Women were drawn to him, and he never lacked for female companionship.

For 1971 he joined John Wyer's potent team of Porsche 917s. Right off the bat, he won the Daytona 24 Hour and the brutal Monza 1000 km. Exactly one week after the French GP (where he'd retired), he drove his friend Herbert Muller's Ferrari at a track new to him. By now he'd raced on virtually all of the big-time tracks; this would be his first time at the lesser Norisring in Nuremberg. To no one's surprise, however, Pedro was leading the 200-mile race. Suddenly a back-marker cut him off, slamming him into a wall, where an explosion of fire enveloped his car. He was eventually dragged from the wreck but did not survive.

Mexico adores its F1 drivers and honors its grand prix history. In memory of Pedro and Ricardo, the track in Mexico City is proudly named *Autódromo Hermanos Rodriguez*, where hard work, piles of pesos, and dedicated people rebuilt the facility and lured the circus back in 2015 after years of calendarensis interruptus.

The Mexican flag that Ricardo and Pedro carried so high is aloft once again in F1.

Even Ferrari drivers have to sit around and wait during race weekend, as here at the 1969 USGP at the Glen. A handful as a racing prodigy, Pedro grew into an endurance legend.

Pedro and designer Aubrey Woods, right, took their Yardley BRM to 10th place in the 30-car Questor GP in 1971.

JODY SCHECKTER
South Africa January 29, 1950

If ever there was a wild child in FI, it was Jody Scheckter. He burst out of the rough-and-tumble style of local South African events when he was 22 and hit the FI road, literally. His crazy lines at speed through corners drew plenty of attention, but not the kind that a driver wants, especially a brand new driver.

His first FI race was the 1972 USGP at Watkins Glen, where he was running third in a Yardley McLaren before he spun out and finished ninth. The 1973 opener, his second race, was his home race in South Africa, where he finished ninth, having skirted a lap two crash that took out Regazzoni and Hailwood. He was leading his third race, the French, when he tangled with Emerson Fittipaldi, putting them both out. His fourth was the British at Silverstone. He qualified sixth and immediately galloped to fourth before crashing mid-pack in the crowded opening lap, thus single-handedly totaling at least seven other cars. The mechanical devastation alone was monumental, the financial cost astronomical, and Surtees driver Andrea de Adamich suffered a broken leg.

The Grand Prix Drivers Association had seen enough. It called Jody in to discuss his driving behavior and, if many drivers got their way, boot him out of FI altogether.

In his corner was GPDA President Denny Hulme and the heavyweight McLaren team. Denny had taken Jody under his wing and they shared quarters from time to time. Each had started out as a mechanic, each had worked on his own car for local races, each had left home hoping to break into big-time racing, and, Jody told me, "both of us arrived off the ship with no shoes on." Insiders called them The Bear and Baby Bear. The upshot of the GPDA meeting, fortunately for Jody, was that Jody was suspended for four FI races, the heart of the 1973 season.

Chatting with me shortly after that fateful meeting, Jody said,

Team Manager Phil Kerr does some coaching at The Glen, 1972, during Jody's rocky entry into F1. Note the alarming degree of a driver's exposure and vulnerability.

Jody's learning curve shot up during the 1973 season, saving a career that had been headed for the dumpster.

TIM SCHENKEN, OAM
Australia September 26, 1943

Tim was a cheery guy whenever I saw him, which was at the beginning of his FI career. Although he drove in FI for five years and was a member of five different major teams and earned a total of seven championship points, it was in endurance racing that he found the most success.

Driving for Ferrari, he twice won the fabled Nurburgring 1000 km. He earned second-place finishes in such other classic races as the Brands Hatch 1000 km, the Watkins Glen 6 Hour, the Sebring 12 Hour, the Zeltweg 1000 km and the Monza 1000 km.

His Formula Three achievements included winning the 1968 British championship in a Brabham, and he did well in Formula Fords and later F2. Porsche was his car of choice toward the end of a career that ended in 1977.

Tim and Howden Ganley added "constructor" to their list of professions when they formed Tiga Race Cars Ltd. in 1974. Tiga open-wheel and sports cars won various races and championships in Europe, Australia and North America over the next 15 years. Tim left the company, though, in 1982 and eventually returned home to Australia with his wife and children.

The love affair Tim had with racing extended far beyond the wheel, beyond even constructorship. In Australia, he moved into race administration, where he quickly earned leadership positions on race committees, boards, commissions, and confederations that organize and support all sorts of race efforts. In addition to all that, which still holds true today, he is Australia's representative to the FIA in Paris.

In June of 2016, Queen Elizabeth II included Tim in her birthday honors, awarding him the Order of Australia Medal for his achievements in motorsports.

Earlier, in 2008, the Confederation of Australian Motor Sports voted Tim a Membership of Honour award[9], given "to a person whose achievements in motor sport have demonstrated leadership, commitment and passion which has added greatly to the value and stature of Australian motor sport."

It can't be said any better than that.

---

9   The inaugural award, given in 1971, went to Tim's hero, Sir Jack Brabham. The honor went to Alan Jones in 1980, the year of his World Championship with Williams.

Tim's F1 career was just starting here at the 1971 Questor GP, where he fought from 14th to 5th. He still officially represents Australia in the world of motor racing.

GEORGES-FRANCIS (JOHNNY) SERVOZ-GAVIN

France (January 18, 1942 - May 29, 2006, Age 64)

Born into wealth, pampered in gilded society and radiating magnetic handsomeness, Johnny looked to have it all. With Grenoble as his hometown, he became a ski instructor in the French Alps, and with his easy charm, he became a French idol who set hearts aflutter.

He started out entering rallies, but quickly wanted more. He went to driving school. He entered F3 races. In 1966 he won the French F3 championship in the French Matra, earning himself an F1 ride in the 1967 Monaco event. That earned him entry in five 1968 grands prix, and he seemed to be fulfilling his potential when at full-tilt Monza he drove his Matra to second place behind Hulme's McLaren and a split second ahead of Ickx's Ferrari.

His schedule in 1969 was packed with both F1 and F2 events. At the wheel of the four-wheel-drive F1 Matra, he picked up a championship point for finishing sixth in the Canadian GP. He had much more success in F2, where he drove off with the European Championship. Invariably he had a warm smile ready for the cameras that were always pointed his way.

At the end of that season he managed to squeeze in some rallying, and that was to be his undoing. During a winter event, a low-hanging tree branch caught him across the face, injuring an eye. He thought all was well as 1970 began: He was Jackie Stewart's teammate on the Ken Tyrrell team, and he earned two more points in the season's second race in Spain. But when he smacked a barrier and failed to qualify for Monaco, he realized that his eyesight was not what he needed it to be. On the spot, he withdrew from the race and hung up his driving gloves.

After that, houseboat living suited him despite an explosion on his canal barge that seriously burned him in 1982. Over the next 24 years, one hopes he maintained his friendships and enjoyed activities, although his health evidently was not good. He had a son by his first wife; he and his second wife had no children.

He died in Grenoble, having circled back to where his very full life had started.

Neither Johnny nor the behatted Ken Tyrrell, right, look overjoyed at the cold, wet practice for the 1969 USGP at Watkins Glen.

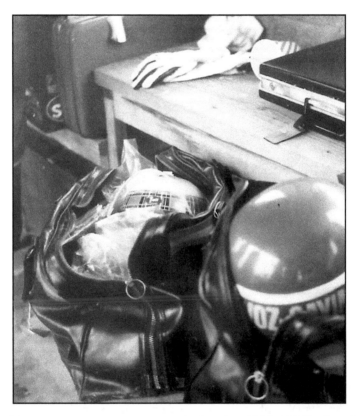

Team Matra accoutrements sit ready for the 1969 USGP. One helmet displays the driver's name. The other just as clearly proclaims its Scottish owner. Such free access around the pits is impossible today.

Johnny's four-wheel drive Matra-Ford finished 7th and last at the 1969 USGP, but he was 16 laps down, rendering the car as Not Classified. He'd scored the 4WD's only point in the Canadian GP at Mosport Park two weeks earlier.

GIUSEPPI (JO, SEPPI) SIFFERT
Switzerland (July 7, 1936 - October 24, 1971, Age 35)

Jo Siffert came up the hard way. In the beginning he earned the money he needed by working in a junkyard, then as an apprentice mechanic, then selling used cars. He finally had enough to buy himself a racing bike, and by 1959 was the Swiss 350 cc champion. Prize monies were enough to buy himself four wheels, a Lotus F3 (then called Formula Junior). In only his second season, he and his Lotus won the Junior European title.

When he turned to Formula One in 1962, he did that the hard way, too, sometimes sleeping in fields near the tracks where on race day he turned heads. After he beat World Champion Jim Clark at a 1964 race in Sicily, one of those who noticed was privateer Rob Walker. Mid-season, Jo found himself racing Rob's Brabhams alongside the established star Jo Bonnier. Siffert promptly ascended the podium at The Glen. Give him good equipment and he just took off, rewarding his team, his growing crowd of fans and himself.

But the next two years saw too many mechanical breakdowns among occasional brilliant finishes. Never tied to one type of racing, Jo meanwhile added endurance racing to his repertoire. So different from the FI side of his career, right from the start his years with Porsche were hugely successful. Paired most often with Brian Redman and later Derek Bell, Jo conquered Daytona, Sebring, Monza, Spa, the Nurburgring, the Targa Florio, Watkins Glen, and on and on.

It didn't take long for the Swiss to elevate Jo to hero status and follow his every race. A plaque in his hometown of Fribourg says it best: Jo Siffert quickly became "the first Swiss legend of modern endurance racing."

Despite his being a Swiss national hero and living legend, I never once saw him throw his weight around or assume he could walk on water. Talking with him was always a pleasant experience. He always *connected*. Rather quiet and with no bluster, his geniality underpinned every conversation. Behind the wheel, though, there was nothing quiet about him and he was lightning fast. No competitor wanted to see him barreling up behind because in a flash he'd be around and gone.

On top of FI and endurance, Jo added the monster Can-Am cars, taking Porsche to strong finishes in the McLaren-Chevrolet era.

He also took the time to make a cameo appearance in the 1967 classic film, *Grand Prix*. And it's said that Jo's buddy Steve McQueen modeled his star character in *Le Mans* on his Swiss friend; Jo had a cameo part in that film, too, which was released in 1971.

The new March FI team looked promising for 1970, so Siffert joined the team that already had World Champion Jackie Stewart. But mechanical gremlins undermined the promise and both drivers changed teams for 1971, Jackie going to Tyrrell and Jo going to Yardley BRM.

The BRM team had an interesting mix of drivers, for there sat Siffert's arch rival in endurance events, Pedro Rodriguez. Two notable additions in mid-August were the brand new Austrian driver, Helmut Marko (Jochen Rindt's partner-in-mischief) and Peter Gethin, who would win the very next race, at Monza. The BRM proved very good for Jo and got better as the year went on. He won the Austrian GP and nearly nipped Cevert at the USGP.

It was another Jackie Stewart year, however, as the Scot gathered up the second of his three World Championships. To honor Stewart, a victory race was staged at Brands Hatch on October 24. Jo took the pole. In an early lap, he and Ronnie Peterson tangled, but each continued. The evidently damaged suspension on Jo's car held up until lap 15, when it gave out at speed. Before the car even stopped, it exploded in flames. With a broken leg, Jo could not get himself out. The first personnel on the scene had fire extinguishers that didn't work. The extinguishers that did work arrived much too late.

Because of his fatal circumstances, on-board fire extinguishers and air piped into driving helmets were almost immediately mandated.

Fifty thousand people including many FI and endurance drivers attended Jo's funeral, and one of his team's Gulf-Porsche 917s led the long and somber caravan of hearse, family and close friends along the streets of Fribourg.

In tribute to his friend Jo, the distinguished Fribourg painter and sculptor Jean Tingley created a mechanical metal fountain that animates a large pond in a Fribourg park. The official canton records list the Jo Siffert Fountain as being "of national significance."

As is the enduring spirit of Jo Siffert.

At The Glen in 1969, Jo wears his uniquely decorated helmet with the Swiss symbol of a white cross on a red background. From early on, he was and still is a Swiss national hero.

Soft-spoken and hard-charging, low-key and high class, Jo gets ready to race his Porsche in the 1971 Can Am at Laguna Seca. He finished 5th. (Also entered were Steve Matchett, who finished 13th in a Porsche, and David Hobbs in a Titanium Chevrolet that DNFd.)

Jo studies the front end of his Can-Am Porsche at Laguna Seca 1971. Nowadays in F1, mechanics would rush to shield such a view from prying eyes and cameras.

JACKIE STEWART, OBE
Scotland June 11, 1939

World Champion once. Twice. *Three* times.

The best driver of his era.

Ranked in the top three of most best-drivers-of-all-time lists (usually just behind Senna and Fangio), and never lower than seventh.

In the first 16 years of the world driving title, only two other men had achieved three championships: Fangio (who won five) and Brabham. It would be 14 more years before another driver reached three (Nelson Piquet in '87).

The details of Jackie Stewart's career, and indeed his whole life so far, are chronicled in great stacks of books and articles:

- How he was so fast and so precise that he attracted attention from the drop of the first flag.

- How as early as his first year in F1, racing author Graham Gauld wrote that Jackie had "achieved more in one year than most racing drivers achieve in 10. Even Jim Clark's meteoric rise was nothing compared to Jackie's progress."

- How reality came literally crashing in on him at Spa '66, when after a wreck he was trapped in his cockpit with gasoline up to his armpits for half an hour with a broken collar bone, a concussion, and an injured kidney. It was then, he told George Plimpton during a 1972 ABC TV Special, that he realized what racing was all about.

- How for 1971, he turned down offers from both Lotus and Ferrari and stayed with Ken Tyrrell.

- How he and Tyrrell took first the Matra and then the Tyrrell to a total of five World Championships—the Constructors titles in 1969 and 1973, and Jackie's personal World Driving Championships in 1969, 1971 and 1973.

The year 1972 didn't get left out of momentous events, and that year typifies the extremes that F1 drivers are subjected to. Queen Elizabeth II awarded Jackie his OBE that year, even before his third championship. It was also the ten-year anniversary of his and beautiful Helen's marriage, augmented by two sons, Paul (1965) and Mark (1968). On the dark side, he lost his father that year while he was racing in Argentina, but the news was kept from him until after the race, which he won. Meanwhile he developed a bleeding ulcer that forced him to suspend activities for several weeks mid-season.

By 1973, he was running on fumes and we could all see that he shouldn't and couldn't possibly go on. But of course he did. Still, unbeknownst to anyone, in April he made the decision to retire at season's end, and he told Ken. But for contractual and other reasons, they kept it a secret. Jackie pushed through to the end, earned his third world title, and on October 14 announced that he was packing it in.

Jackie was and still is a high profile personality. *Time* magazine very early described him as "the flippant, flamboyant Scot." I was privileged to be around that young Jackie, when he was bouncy and loud and uninhibited and tons of fun. His whirlwind energy seemed to bubble up from his natural optimism. Laughter and excitement of his own making swirled around him and enveloped everyone close by. However, as the seasons rolled on he quieted some, and he became clearly weighted down by the terrible losses the blood sport inflicted.

He was a master racer, yet he had even greater impact outside the cockpit. Because of Jackie, Formula One was changed forever in two areas:

One, he became a gadfly for improving racing safety. He tackled everybody and everything from driving suits to trackside barriers to car equipment. His popularity among other drivers dipped occasionally because he kept the pressure on; not all of them felt that risk needed so much handling. But Jackie was and still is persistent, vocal and influential.

He had a doctor at every race. He had a jet standing by that was equipped with patient oxygen. He had burn doctors, neurosurgeons, and others all over Europe on an hour's call. He had rescue directions painted on his car in three languages. As he told Dave Kindred of the *Washington Post,* "I knew when the season started every January, I would have two major accidents that year with the potential to be seriously injured or killed. It was up to me to minimize the extent of the injury, to assure the least amount of vulnerability."

A *Time* article dated August 1, 1969 says, "He was among the first Grand Prix drivers to use the six-point-contact seatbelt, and he introduced the idea of remote-control fire extinguishers in the engine compartment and cockpit, which racing authorities may make compulsory." You can look at the record books and see how many drivers would have been saved in the next years had these devices been in full use.

Each new dreadful racing death—and by his count, he lost 57 friends to racing accidents—revealed another area needing Jackie's safety spotlight. In a way, the increased safety of open-wheel racing eased out the daredevils and beckoned the technicians. That simplifies it way too much (I doubt that Jack Brabham, for example, thought of himself as a daredevil), but do some comparisons yourself: Stirling Moss contrasted with Michael Schumacher; Jochen Rindt with Lewis Hamilton. They just don't seem to be cut from the same cloth. The super-tech level of today requires a different skill set than those earlier and deadly years.

Two, Jackie saw that being an F1 race driver had enormous commercial potential. Stirling Moss had taken the first tiny steps in this direction, but Jackie boosted it to professional heights. He realized that the drivers themselves could be a huge draw for both sponsors and ticket-buyers. To the best of my knowledge, he was the first to get professional representation, signing with Mark McCormack's International Management Group (IMG) in 1969. (Bernie Ecclestone later saw that F1 was a product in itself, one that could be publicized to draw the sponsors who could keep the money rolling in.)

Jackie crafted himself into a man at ease in front of a thousand cameras, in front of prying microphones, in front of crowds big and small. He's a marvelous interview, partly because of his always-ready personality, partly because he always has facts and opinions and knows how to deliver them. With me at least, he never rushed scheduled interviews, acting like he had all the time in the world, when in fact there were impatient clankings and shufflings just outside his door. He was so cooperative and engaging, in fact, that it sometimes took a beat to realize that he has as strong a will and as total a self-discipline as the flinty Graham Hill.

Those characteristics helped propel the Stewart FI team created and run by Jackie and his son Paul. The Stewart-Fords raced in smaller formulae before entering FI, where the team survived for three memorable years, 1997-1999.

Jackie's wife, Helen, has been his support and companion over this past half century and counting. Always an elegant presence, her serious health problems these days have wrought major changes in their lives.

Neither retired nor retiring, however, Jackie still works on behalf of racing safety, is still involved in the business side of racing, still shares his exuberance. In 2001, he was knighted by Queen Elizabeth II, whose grandsons occasionally turn up at grands prix. Both of Jackie's sons have been involved in various aspects of motor racing, with Paul donning driver's helmet, owner's cap, and manager's mantle.

Lady Helen and Sir Jackie have nine grandchildren, with one of them—Dylan—looking to be the latest Stewart in the Stewart racing dynasty.

If ever a man wrested change from the frozen jaws of the FI status quo, it's Jackie Stewart. He will have left the sport not as he found it, but as he shaped it, colored it and changed it for the better, forever and for all.

Two highly focused independent souls prepare for the 1969 USGP at The Glen, although Jackie in his Matra had already clinched the world title (a good thing, too, because the Matra expired early).

Jackie had reason to smile at the 1971 Questor GP: He and Bud Stanner of IMG, left, would take personal publicity and endorsements to new and lucrative heights that are still soaring today.

The toll of personal risk and losing so many friends shows on Jackie's face by 1971, and how could it not? Still, he raced until retiring at the end of the 1973 season.

Bareheaded for a rare moment, Jackie would win the 1972 USGP and lead the Tyrrell team to a dominating finish with Cevert in 2ⁿᵈ and Depailler in 7ᵗʰ.

JOHN SURTEES, OBE
England (February 11, 1934 – March 10, 2017, Age 83)

John Surtees was one of the nicest and warmest drivers to chat with. He didn't double-talk or play word games. His eyes would light up and he smiled a lot when he was enjoying the conversation. He seemed almost totally devoid of guile, and he did not play life in a cool way. Those warm, limpid eyes could turn stone cold in an instant. He was a study in pronounced contrasts: Gracious and blunt. Warm and cold. Robust and frail. Jolly and grim. A team player with his own drummer. A sociable loner. Pleasant and ill-tempered.

His career, too, ran the gamut. He started out winning on two wheels and ended up a champion on four. He raced in F1, Can Am and endurance, forging a full career as a driver before making his mark as a constructor.

Whatever he turned his hand to, he tended to hit hard and fast. His rise in motorcycle racing was immediate: At age 17, he gave established stars fits by running right with them and sometimes beating them. When he was 22, he won his first world title. Through his mid-20's, he piled on six more two-wheel world championships for a total of seven.

At age 26 he decided to try four wheels. In only his second grand prix he finished second, then in his third he grabbed the pole. He raced for Reg Parnell's Cooper, followed by Lola. He ranked fourth in only his third year in F1.

Ferrari couldn't resist! It snapped him up starting with the 1963 season. In return, John didn't mess around. He promptly won his first Ferrari race, the Sebring 12 Hour. At the end of his second year with Ferrari, he won Enzo Ferrari his second International Cup for F1 Manufacturers[10] in six years (Phil Hill won the first in 1961) and himself the 1964 World Driving Championship. John and the *Commendatore*

---

10   Now the World Constructors Championship

got along famously, spending long laughter-filled lunches together. John quickly grew to adore Italy and all things Italian, and Ferrari fans felt it. *Il Grande John* was beloved by the *tifosi*.

The next year was nearly his last. With Ferrari's permission, he was set to race a Can-Am Lola at the Canadian Mosport circuit. In practice there on September 25, he was terribly injured when his car broke and he crashed. He was not expected to survive. Despite missing the last two races, he ranked fifth in a season dominated by Jim Clark, Graham Hill, Jackie Stewart and Dan Gurney.

When the 1966 season opened, who should materialize on the grid but Big John in his team Ferrari. He won a non-championship grand prix at Syracuse in April. In May at Monaco, he earned a front-row slot beside pole-sitter Clark; he was leading the physically demanding race when mechanical failure ended his day. In June at Spa, he took the pole, the fastest lap *and* the race victory.

Less than a week later, Ferrari Team Manager Eugenio Dragoni deemed team leader John not recovered enough from his Canada injuries to drive in Le Mans! It's a long, complicated and conflicted story, as everything tends to be with *Scuderia Ferrari*, but the upshot was that John, who'd worked unbelievably hard to get himself back in shape, who'd then won a big race in April, led an even bigger one in May, and won the grueling Spa in June, decided that if he wasn't "fit enough" for Ferrari, then Ferrari wasn't fit enough for him, and he walked.

Not one to let things fester, John swiftly took another action. Just three days after Le Mans, John strode through the Ferrari factory gate and met with Enzo privately. As A.J. Baime describes it in *Go Like Hell,* pp. 246-47, " . . only Surtees and Ferrari would ever fully know" what was discussed, but "the two agreed they would have to part ways." There would be no going back.

Except for their unfortunate split, who knows what the two of them together might have achieved . . .

John ran the rest of the season in a team Cooper, coming in second at the Nurburgring and winning the Mexican GP. Were it not for the Ferrari team chopping John off, he quite likely would have won his second world championship. As it was, he finished second to Jack Brabham, who clinched his third title.

With Honda over the next two years, John won the 1967 Italian GP. Period. There were to be no more victories at the wheel. An unremarkable 1969 with BRM was followed by still another major career shift: John eased over the pit wall to the constructors' side, and in 1970 presented F1 with a new marque, the Surtees. The two team cars were driven primarily by Mike Hailwood and then Tim Schenken in F1. They also competed in F2, where Hailwood won the 1972 European Championship, leaving an indelible mark for the Surtees marque.

The finances and logistics and demands of running a Formula One team are enormous, and John proved himself over and over during the life of the Surtees operation. But at the conclusion of the 1978 season, this part of John's life finally came to a close.

He stayed active in historic racing events, and he maintained a fantastic collection of vintage motorcycles. He and his second wife Jane raised two daughters and a son, Henry, who was a lifelong racer.

There is no greater blow than the death of one's child, and Henry was killed in an F2 racing accident at Brands Hatch in 2009 when he was just 18. Words are hopelessly inadequate to describe what John and his family endured. Turning their tragedy into a positive force, they formed the Henry Surtees Foundation, which focuses on road safety programs, equipment and facilities for injured race drivers, and other areas of safer motor sports.

Once a Ferrari driver, always a Ferrari driver, and with the passage of time and personnel, John and the Ferrari folks eventually put their troubles behind them. Until nearly the end, John went on various public-appearance jaunts on behalf of Ferrari. John forever deeply loved Italy, and the *tifosi* forever loved *Il Grande John*. He elicited rousing cheers when he appeared on the Monza 2013 podium to interview race winner Sebastian Vettel; another former Ferrari driver, Jean Alesi, interviewed second-place Fernando Alonso and third-place Mark Webber.

An anecdote from March 2016 illustrates the strength of the Surtees character. For the Race of Champions at Brands Hatch (England), John fielded a Team Surtees FI car to be driven by World Champion Alan Jones. One of the car's sponsors was a prophylactic manufacturer—which sent the BBC into conniptions to the point where it demanded John remove the adverts from the car. You can guess his reaction! So the BBC refused to televise the race and that was that. (It's just as in character that when the same car with the same markings raced later that year at Long Beach in the United States, CBS-TV covered the event with no fuss whatsoever.)

John was tough, without question, but he wasn't always physically strong. Exactly one year later, respiratory failure finally overcame him and he died in hospital just as spring was coming.

Tributes poured in from the whole racing universe, mourning the loss of one of the greatest men in motor sports. The name John Surtees is permanently embedded in the proudest annals of motor racing history.

At Watkins Glen in 1969, John savors a quiet moment alone in the paddock, his own Surtees marque already taking shape back home.

Ahead of Jo Bonnier, John wears the Surtees game face as he emerges from the drivers meeting just before the 1969 USGP, where John's BRM would share the podium with first-time winner Jochen Rindt and Piers Courage in 2ⁿᵈ.

John encourages Tim Schenken at the redesigned Watkins Glen circuit in 1972, the year the Surtees marque with Mike Hailwood would win the F2 European Championship. Over the nine seasons they raced, Surtees FI cars would amass an impressive 53 championship points.

Race day at the 1972 USGP finds John striding through the pits, head in charging mode, hands clenched. Tensions ratchet up all week to unbelievable pressure by Sunday afternoon.

REINE WISELL
Sweden September 30, 1941

This smiling Swede had a busy career in the 1970s, entering F1 and F2 races, endurance events, the Can-Am series and others around the world. He drove Lotuses, Porsches, Lolas, Surteeses, Camaros, whenever and wherever. His Swedish F3 championship in 1967 eventually took him to F2 and in 1970, into F1.

Colin Chapman was still reeling from the death of Jochen Rindt at Monza that year, but he had a team to run. He selected Wisell for the United States and the Mexican grands prix. Wisell's first F1 race was also his best finish, a third in the USGP at Watkins Glen. It was to be the only F1 podium of his career.

He stayed with Lotus another year before moving to BRM for most of 1972. One grand prix in '73 and one in '74 brought his F1 experience to a close. Several F2 races for the Surtees team in 1974, and his F2 years were over.

Wisell was destined to come off second to Ronnie Peterson for Swedish attention, and second to Emerson Fittipaldi for Lotus recognition. He retired on a high note, however, when in 1975 he won the European GT title in a Porsche.

He has taught advanced driving techniques and advises up-and-coming Swedish drivers.

To the best of my knowledge, he's based in Thailand these days.

Reine, center, ponders a Lotus problem with Emerson Fittipaldi, left, and mechanic Eddie Dennis. The body language is prescient, because neither driver made it even halfway through the 1971 Questor GP.

BONUS SECTION

The Team Owners/
Constructors

INTRODUCTION

What of the men who made the cars that killed the men who drove them?

They shared with their drivers the finely-honed gene for competition, the driving need to be the best in an arena of their choosing. They needed to win, and they had the skills and the knowledge to build, rather than drive, their way to the top. In addition, they were seized by curiosity—how fast can I make it go? How far can I stretch the materials? Can I push past the limits? Every fresh idea meant a new boundary to seek and exceed.

Several had engineering degrees, and all had engineering savvy. A few started out as racing drivers themselves but rather quickly realized their limitations as drivers compared with the unlimited and visionary possibilities in creating cars for others to race.

The marques wrought by Brabham, McLaren, Gurney, Mosley, Stewart and Surtees evolved after their FI driving careers and are already covered in each driver's section. The five team owners/ constructors in this section took a different path but ended up in the same place: part of the complex and historic fabric of Formula One.

Obviously, constructors don't make cars so they kill people. But they do make cars that kill. A fatal F1 accident ends a life that until one single instant was bubbling with talent and skill and goals and high spirit. The sudden snuffing of that spark is terrible enough. But a fatal accident can also start a chain of reactions that rattle far down the corridors of time. In Italy, for example, every conceivable person involved in a race fatality gets charged with a variety of crimes and hauled into court. Cases can drag on for years. Sometimes team members do not go back until the case is cleared for fear of being arrested. And if a state doesn't pursue legal action against a constructor, mechanic, team manager, et al., a driver's family sometimes takes the team to court. Some cases are won, some are lost, but they put everybody through more hell than they've already been through with the driver's death.

Single-car fatal racing accidents are rarely caused, I believe, by driver error. Most—and I have no scientific research to back this—are caused by mechanical failure. A wheel came off, the suspension broke, the steering gave out. It seems inherent in the system that things will break; that's the nature of any complex mechanism, be it an airplane, a nuclear plant or a race car. But so horrifying is a fatal accident that blame is sought and placed.

Constructors obviously react differently to the death of one of their drivers. Some grow family-close to a driver, like Colin Chapman and Jim Clark; when Jim died, it very nearly crushed Chapman. At the other end of the scale, some builders regard their drivers more as valued but replaceable parts of their fabulous machines.

Whatever the degree of distress, the show must go on. So a new driver is flown in, strapped into the cockpit and sent off. The whole purpose of building a racer was and is to create a car that will go faster longer than those of their competitors. Their goal was and is to win the Constructors World Championship.

Throughout the early years (1958 saw the first Constructors title), prestige was the only reward for winning that championship. My car can go faster than your car; my boys are better than yours; etc. There was little television coverage, let alone TV revenue to be shared with the teams. The constructors had no organization of their own, no leverage, no cohesion. What clout racing people had was vested in the Grand Prix Drivers Association, which was hardly an advocate for team owners' concerns. Thus was born the Formula One Constructors Association (FOCA), which hoped to be the tail that wagged the dog; eventually this morphed into the Formula I Teams' Association. But there was a bigger dog in the pack (hello, Bernie Eccle$tone—a whole other story), and FOTA disbanded in February 2014. The constructors refused to be voiceless for long, though, and soon the "Big Five" formed the elite Strategy Group, with Ferrari as the most privileged of the privileged, followed by Mercedes, Red Bull, and McLaren, with Williams catching the crumbs. Today, the rest of the teams are allowed to attend some of the meetings but have no say.

Winning the Constructors title brings the advantages of attracting better drivers, getting more press coverage, luring heftier sponsor money, drawing more skilled employees, creating a stronger brand—which in some cases then boost sales of their road cars to the public. Every single championship point means big bucks in the team bank account at the end of the season. The bounty for winning all the marbles, the Constructors World Championship, has rocketed to *hundreds of millions* of dollars. Each year.

Some constructors were engineers—Colin Chapman and Bruce McLaren, for example. Some had tinkered with cars all their early lives—Dan Gurney comes to mind. Some were top drivers before they hopped the pit wall into the garage—Brabham, Surtees and Stewart are good examples. All but Louis Stanley in the next section had their early dreams of becoming big-time race drivers butt up against the reality that their will was there but not their skill. Somewhere along the line, each one managed to scrape up enough money to start actually building a car themselves.

From there, the journey to the top came one race, one debt, one hour at a time. So gargantuan was the struggle that few attempted it and even fewer survived. In addition to grit and energy and skill and money and time, to reach the top took and still takes vision, patience, leadership, creativity and perspective and on and on.

Nowadays, only major consortiums and manufacturers even contemplate getting into F1. It costs vast piles of money to assemble a brain trust, attract the right team at the right time in the right place, lure good drivers—and do it all on speculation. Behemoths like Mercedes and Honda and Renault have come and gone, and come again.

Another big change that has evolved is the virtual disappearance of the single designer, one person who designs the whole vehicle. Adrian Newey is perhaps the last practitioner. In recent years, specialization has taken over, and too often the sum is not even *as* great as the parts.

When it works, it's the top of the world. Sponsor money floods in, the media flocks around, the team name is suddenly a household word, drivers become stars, the brand soars.

But there can come a time when it doesn't work anymore. The formula changes . . . a bad decision is made . . . the money dwindles . . . key minds depart . . . stuff happens. Recently, for example, the roaring Red Bull was unceremoniously knocked from its perennial perch by the renascent Mercedes. Fabled Ferrari keeps hemorrhaging internally only to rise again. Mighty McLaren has sunk halfway down the standings. Williams seems to live on a perpetual roller coaster. Sad ends awaited the heroic teams of Brabham and Tyrrell and Lotus. The Surtees and Stewart operations finally had to cut their losses and move on. And so it goes.

That's what books like this are for—to record and remember the great names that once flourished and enriched the sport, and to support what Formula One is today. Each team has left stories and memories and records that are indelible in the history of the most elite motor sport in the world.

THE TEAM OWNERS/ CONSTRUCTORS

Colin Chapman

Louis Stanley

Ken Tyrrell

Rob Walker

Frank Williams

COLIN CHAPMAN, CBE
England (May 19, 1928 - December 16, 1982, Age 54)

Colin Chapman was Lotus and Lotus was Colin Chapman. The man was brilliant, arrogant and hands-on. He innovated, irritated, improved and influenced. From 1956 until his death, every project he touched bore his genius, whether in materials, power-to-weight ratios, chassis structure, strut placement, etc. To those of us in FI back then, he and Lotus were eternal forces.

We were wrong on both counts. Of course, we were. Nothing lasts forever (well, maybe Ferrari).

In the beginning, there was a stable. That's where, in North London in 1952, Chapman located the workshop for his brand new Lotus Engineering Company, fueled by £25 from his wife, Hazel. His calendar was already jammed with race meetings where he himself took the wheel of various racers and his own earliest prototypes; *brio* best describes his driving style. By then he already had an engineering degree and was drawn to both structural and aeronautical engineering. The ingredients for all that followed were securely in place.

During the next few years, he continued driving (he even made the Vanwall team), consulting (for Vanwall and BRM), and developing his own racers that he sold to others (the Lotus 7 started a whole dynasty). So busy and super-efficient was he that he wore mechanic's overalls to races, the quicker to lay waste to any problems.

The first Lotus single-seater was a 1956 F2 car. The first rear-engine Lotus emerged in FI in 1960. That year he also drove a Jaguar to victory in the touring car race held in conjunction with the British GP.

He was a super-quick learner and felt that time was always pushing him. He learned to fly in nothing flat so he could save travel time. He learned accounting over a Friday and Saturday and took over Lotus' business books the next Monday morning. Even more useful in a sport obsessed with speed and outrunning one's competitors, he had a swift turn-around time from idea to working drawing.

The Lotus racers that he sold grew so popular that he had to turn away customers. He curtailed his own driving so he could concentrate on building not only formula racers and Indy 500 cars but road cars as well. Note that his very first visit to Indianapolis, in 1963 with Jim Clark, produced a stunning second place that would've, perhaps should've, been the win.

In any gathering, at any event or meeting, even in any conversation, Chapman *prevailed*. He had a presence that could not be ignored or upstaged. Every argument/discussion/debate was his to win, and he did. He was a success and he knew it. Everything was humming, zipping along nicely at top speed.

Then to crown the whole thing, along came a shy moody farm boy named Jim Clark.

The Chapman-Clark bond was an added propellant for Lotus, as though any were needed. Their uncanny technical communication further speeded development of the Lotus formula cars, and Jim's unearthly skills behind the wheel boosted Lotus right to the top. In 1963 and again in 1965, Jim's efforts won him the World Driving Championship and the Constructors title for Lotus. Some of Clark's records have only recently been eclipsed and some still stand today, half a century later—and kindly note that there are over twice as many races these days. That special bond between geniuses proved cautionary, however, because when Jim was killed in 1968, the personal loss so devastated Chapman that he came *this* close to quitting the whole thing. He himself said that after Jim's death, he never viewed racing the same. Chapman's colleagues go a step further, stating that Chapman was a different man personally, before Jim's loss and after it.

Somehow, though, Chapman managed to regroup, and over the next years with Graham Hill, Jochen Rindt, Emerson Fittipaldi and Mario Andretti he would win five more World Constructors Championships.

But the top isn't called the pinnacle for nothing. By definition, a pinnacle is a small spire, a pointed tip. Balancing there is precarious, and the fall is steep. Despite having won a towering stack of world titles, by 1980 Lotus was gasping for its financial breath: Failures such as the F1 four-wheel drive and ground-effects Lotuses were major setbacks; costs were skyrocketing; race-world politics proved both disappointing and distracting. An alliance with Toyota came to nothing, and the foggy relationship with John DeLorean's project led to major problems.

More black clouds loomed as some of those business practices and associations came under legal fire. The storm and whatever its aftermath never arrived, however, because early on a December morning in 1982, Anthony Colin Bruce Chapman died of a sudden heart attack.

His death prevented a possible trashing of his legacy, but it doomed Lotus to a string of labyrinthine legal maneuverings and owners ranging from General Motors to Bugatti to a Malaysian car company. The fabled marque today is owned by the Geely Holding Group based in Hangzhou, China.

Chapman's son Clive oversees the superb car collection, rare artifacts and deep history of the original Lotus, and he is now the keeper of the flame that burned so bright for so long.

Chapman's closeness to Jim Clark exemplified the upside and the dark side of friendships in the killing fields. Chapman was still deeply grieving here at the 1969 USGP.

Chapman examines his handiwork at the Questor GP. Lotus' seven Constructors championships in 15 seasons bested—at the time—a McLaren title almost every three years and Ferrari every four and a half.

The Lotus elite—Emmo Fittipaldi, left, Team Manager Peter Warr, center, and mechanic Eddie Dennis, right—stand by while Chapman thinks up a solution to an unexpected problem at the 1972 USGP.

A mystery for all time is why Chapman, shown here at the 1972 USGP, named his marque Lotus. And he took to his grave why Lotus road car models all start with E: Elan, Exige, Esprit, etc.

LOUIS STANLEY
England (January 6, 1912 - January 8, 2004, Age just 92)

Not for Louis Stanley the sweat of designing or the grease of the BRM workshops—he *owned* the team, he kept to the upper reaches. After all, he'd come from managing the refined Dorchester Hotel in London to marrying into the raucous, over-the-top circus that is Formula One.

Three years after its first grand prix entry, BRM got its first victory when Jo Bonnier out-drove everybody at the 1959 Dutch GP. The same race three seasons later launched Graham Hill's drive to glory when he won the 1962 World Constructors Championship for BRM and the first of two World Driving titles for himself (his second came in a Lotus). And for three seasons after that, BRM finished second in the Constructors race.

After those heady years of the mid-'60s though, BRM amassed an entirely different history. BRM became its own worst enemy. Louis Stanley managed a team that seemed forever time-challenged and struggling. Fine designers like Aubrey Woods and Tony Rudd worked their magic to little avail on cars that chronically proved too slow, too heavy and too late.

Across 22 seasons, BRM brought home 17 grand prix wins, 10 of them at the hands of Graham Hill and two with Jackie Stewart. The remaining five came one each from Bonnier, Siffert, Pedro Rodriguez, Gethin and Beltoise. That's no small potatoes, but one might expect more of a big factory team during the long stretch from their first GP entry in 1956 to their last in 1977.

Stanley's wife, Jean, was the sister of Sir Alfred Owens, owner of British Racing Motors. As Sir Alfred decreased his management, Louis took up the slack and eventually became chairman of the whole business.

He insisted on being addressed as *"Mister* Stanley" (a mark of dignity and honor in England), prompting the irrepressible Dan Gurney to come up with "Big Lou," a moniker that caught on immediately. Stanley did exquisitely set himself up for such responses by, shall we say, putting on airs. He maintained an unflinching aristocratic bearing. He wore an imposing expression on a large head atop a substantial corpus. Throw in an authoritarian manner and long-winded bombast, and he could blast past all manner of obstacles perceived and otherwise.

He went to considerable lengths to keep his personal heritage secret, leading to some tall tales and curious lapses from him about his background. After his death, however, out popped the secret that his father was said to have been former Prime Minister Asquith—a believable claim because his mother was known to have been the PM's mistress. Adding to the now-it-can-be-told revelations, in 2012 came ugly family accusations. I suppose not many F1 people will admit to actually reading *Conspiracy of Secrets* by Stanley's step-daughter, Bobbie Neate, but some probably mulled the claims therein.

Somewhere there is a photo I've seen of ten lithe athlete-drivers relaxing in their swim trunks on beach towels on a vast sunny lawn. In their midst hunkers Stanley in a great dark three-piece suit, looking like a water buffalo amongst fauns. The man unwittingly just begged for balloon-puncturing jabs when the many opportunities presented themselves.

On the other hand, Big Lou became a driving force behind the imperative to increase racing safety, loudly siding with the Jackie Stewart group's push against so many needless racing deaths. *Mister* Stanley's ability to push aside impediments served the cause very well. He himself tested a new fireproof driving suit, enduring 30 seconds of fiery hell to prove its capabilities. His efforts made possible the fully equipped Grand Prix Medical Unit that he arranged to have at every circuit starting in 1967. Not every medical doctor agreed to its need, however; some felt that getting an injured driver directly and immediately to an official hospital was in the driver's best interests.

After a few seasons, the unit drifted into history, but Big Lou and his ideas and techniques helped move FI safety features substantially forward.

BRM eventually shrank into the shadows, a victim of too few successes to draw sustaining sponsors. As for Louis himself, he nimbly switched careers, writing knowledgeably and extensively about racing, including valuable annuals that for many years covered each season's FI racing.

Motor racing has much to thank him for, whether he's remembered as Mister Stanley or as Big Lou.

Stanley with his wife, Jean, at the 1969 USGP in Watkins Glen, N.Y. He headed BRM, but his racing books and magazine columns might be his most lasting legacy.

KEN TYRRELL
England (May 3, 1924 - August 25, 2001, Age 77)

Uncomplicated, direct, free of airs, that was Ken Tyrrell. He wasn't stylish, he wasn't smooth, he had no GQ factor. He was just plenty effective.

Academic endeavors were definitely not his cuppa. Technical school rejected his application, in fact. After a stint in the RAF as a flight engineer, he and his brother established a timber business. Their woodyard featured a big shed with a blue door, behind which he conducted timber affairs while he dreamed of a different sort of career. One outing to a British GP and he'd been smitten: He would become a race driver.

But several factors worked against him. First of all, he was a big fellow and wide-bodied, when the makers of race cars strove to limit size and weight in both their cars and their drivers. And second, Ken had a mind of his own and didn't hesitate to express himself. He seemed a square peg in a round hole—yet when he talked others usually listened.

So where did he fit? As a team owner, of course. He knew cars, he knew drivers, he had a bit of money, and the woodyard was spacious enough to accommodate a second business. In 1960, the Tyrrell Racing Organisation entered its first race. Owner Ken started out in F Junior and worked his way up through F3 and F2, all the while keeping his sights on F1.

Enter Jabby Crombac,[11] the Swiss who was into everything concerned with motor racing—journalist, promoter, race steward. He knew everyone who counted, from Jim Clark to the CEO of Matra, the French engine manufacturer. Jabby arranged for Tyrrell to meet that CEO, and the two of them immediately found that they spoke the same racing language. The result was Team Tyrrell fielding Matra cars

---

11   Gérard Crombac (1929-2005)

starting in 1965. Two years later Ken ran Matras in F1.

One of his F2 Matra drivers especially caught Ken's eye for bigger things, so he invited young Jackie Stewart to test for the F1 team. Jackie hesitated; he was new, he was still feeling his way along. But Stewart's good buddy Jimmy Clark persuaded him that Ken was the man he should drive for if he could.

"My first impression of Ken Tyrrell," Jackie relates in *Winning is Not Enough*, "was of an authoritative man who was absolutely practical and clear about what he wanted to achieve. There were no airs and graces about him at all, and I liked that."

Thus was born a partnership that lasted the entire length of Stewart's dazzling career.

Ken ran his team like a family business, which it literally was. Norah, his wife, supplied support and sandwiches; his two sons helped out as they grew into manhood. Figuratively, too, the team was the same as family. Stewart, for example, didn't have a written contract; a handshake sealed their arrangement. Far ahead of his time, Ken gave team employees pension plans and medical insurance. They showed their appreciation with career-long loyalty and top-notch skills.

Putting on a big show was not Ken's way. When Team Tyrrell arrived at a race, the whole contingent consisted of Ken, Norah, the two drivers and six mechanics. Under Ken's no-nonsense leadership, Team Tyrrell's Matra-Ford won the 1969 Constructors title and Stewart the driving title.

When a winning combination finally clicks into place, changing those ingredients is not a sensible thing to do. However, factors beyond Ken's control came into play for 1970 and a major change had to be wrought. The Matra factory decided to go all-French and produce a French engine for 1970. Stewart tested the new car and found it wanting. On Jackie's word, Ken ended his relationship with Matra and instead went with the new March.

The season proved disastrous on all levels. The March car was a bust. And by the end of the year, three top drivers had been killed—Piers Courage, Bruce McLaren and Jochen Rindt. The season sank into a dark wasteland.

Tyrrell scuttled behind that blue door in his woodyard and emerged with his own marque, the Tyrrell. Stewart drove it brilliantly straight through the 1971 season to another double championship—Constructors and Driving. Jackie would earn his third title in 1973, but Lotus still showed life and took the Constructors title.

Stewart, though, was undergoing changes and at the end of 1973 he packed away his helmet. He would eventually return as an owner/constructor from 1996 until he sold out to Jaguar at the end of 1999. (To continue the story, Jaguar then raced through the 2004 season before selling out to Red Bull. The beat goes on.)

Ken soldiered on through the '80s and into the '90s, but never regained the successes of his earlier years. He struggled against the rising costs of FI, where the onslaught of changing formulae and rocketing costs eventually hammered him until he finally had to give up. In 1999 he sold his Tyrrell team to British American Racing, BAR, which in turn became the Honda team in 2005, then the Ross Brawn team in 2009, and since 2011 the Mercedes behemoth. (The beat . . .)

Ken was figuratively and literally a lumbering man. He made his goals and intentions unflinchingly clear, and he got where he was going by tireless work and tough-love leadership. He railed against the squeezing out of small teams like his, but he couldn't slow the deep-pockets beast that FI had evolved into.

After pancreatic cancer claimed Ken in 2001, FI people packed his funeral service in the Guildford Cathedral, where Dame Kiri Te Kanawa sang in his honor. Outdoors, four Tyrrells formed a mute display of witness and respect for a great name in racing annals.

Tyrrell finds another use for tires as he crams in a bit of paperwork at the Questor GP. Stewart's Tyrrell would finish second overall to Andretti's you-know-what (the "f" word in some circles then and now).

ROB WALKER
British (August 14, 1917 - April 29, 2002, Age 84)

Smooth, quiet, impeccably gliding through the paddock, always a gentleman, Rob Walker chose the roughest path imaginable through Formula One: that of a privateer. Robert Ramsey Campbell Walker's elegant exterior encased an indomitable will that found a way around every impediment.

The racing bug bit little Rob when he was taken to a local race at age seven, and he never recovered. He spent much of his childhood driving around the family estate in Wiltshire, scaring the wits out of his mother (his father died when Rob was three). As a teen he was able to buy better and faster cars, enter local races and horrify her even more.

WW II disrupted what looked to be the colorful career of a high-spirited racing driver. Through six long war years, 1939-1945, Rob flew a wide variety of war planes for the Royal Navy, despite having had his civilian pilot's license cancelled because of adventurous flying.

As the world began its post-war recovery, Rob promised his new wife and family that he would no longer compete in the dangerous formula races. Instead, he began to taste the satisfactions of fielding a racer that someone else drove.

He was born and raised in England, but he carried Scotland in his blood. He was heir to the Johnny Walker whisky empire[12], and in honor of this heritage, he broke out a racing livery that boasted the dark blue of Scotland, usually with white on or around the nose of the car.

Starting with just a toe in the water, he bought near-relics to enter in local events. Then less-old cars in bigger English races. By 1956, he plunged into the European scene with an F1 Cooper. It was a bold move by a man who trusted his own instincts implicitly, because John

---

12   Johnny Walker is still a sponsor in Formula One.

Cooper's little cars drew snickers when they would pull up beside the big Maseratis and Ferraris on the grid. But Rob's driver, young Stirling Moss, soon made the racing fraternity sit up and take notice by giving the factory teams all kinds of trouble. At the Argentine Grand Prix of 1958, Moss beat the whole pack of big boys for the very first F1 victory by a private entrant—and Moss being Moss even then, he did it stuck in second gear most of the race. In the very next event, at glittering Monaco, French war hero Maurice Trintignant snatched the victory in Rob's second Cooper. The RRC Walker Team had arrived.

Rob grew friend-close with nearly all his drivers, but he quickly learned the excruciating price one paid for that in grand prix. In 1962, first Stirling Moss' career ended in a still-unexplained crash in April; that November, a local driver, Gary Hocking, was killed in a Walker Lotus practicing for the South African GP at Natal; and in December, Ricardo Rodriguez died in his Walker Lotus at the Mexican GP. Each loss staggered Rob, and it proved too heavy a burden. At the end of the season, he quit.

But over the winter, the racing bug stirred to life and would not be denied. For 1963, Rob took the Swedish sophisticate Jo Bonnier onto Team Walker.

Around the Walker garage there were few alarums, not a lot of chatter, and as little drama as possible. Rob himself was soft-spoken with a calming presence, and his team reflected its boss. Intense? Oh, yes. Focused? You bet. But the overall atmosphere was one of concentration, get the job done, make it work, without any distracting *sturm und drang*.

Rob didn't hang instructions out on his pit board, didn't give his drivers orders. He left them alone, believing that they knew what to do. And they did, bringing him 149 championship points and nine grand epreuve victories over the years. Names now legendary all found a place with his team: Stirling Moss, Maurice Trintignant, Jo Bonnier, Jo Siffert, Graham Hill.

It could be said that Rob was racing's most prominent minimalist.

He intensely disliked paperwork and kept it to the barest amount possible. Likewise, Team Walker would arrive at a circuit modestly, with just two or three mechanics, Rob himself, and a team manager who doubled as the transporter driver. (Compare this with the mob that BRM or Ferrari, for example, would show up with.)

For ten years, from 1956-1966, F1 circuits saw Rob's entries of Coopers, Lotuses and Brabhams. But the financial monster that grand prix became was gaining on him. By 1966, Rob had to take on a partner, entrepreneur Jack Durlacher. The two carried on for five more seasons but were finally forced to fold their tent at the end of 1970. Rob shifted what sponsor support he had to the Surtees team for several years until finally retiring in 1974.

Today, the very idea of a team in F1 without major factory backing has pretty much gone the way of clutch pedals and five speeds. Costs have simply grown too high. After Rob, it would be 20 years before a viable independent team ventured into F1 again: Eddie Jordan and his team colorfully survived from 1991 through 2004. Peter Sauber had support for the first few years, 1993-2010, then ran as an independent until selling in 2017; his name stayed with the team until the 2019 season, when the team was renamed Alfa Romeo. At a bare-bones minimum, it costs some $6M to run *just one race,* and it goes way up from there. As the saying goes, How do you make a small fortune? Answer: You start with a large fortune and go motor racing.

After his career as a driver, Rob had switched to being an owner. After the team's demise in 1970, he switched again, this time from owner to journalist. Through the next decades he wrote on all aspects of F1 racing past and present for *Road & Track* magazine. If ever a man knew racing inside and out, top to bottom, side to side and back again, it was Rob Walker. He took racing, and racing took him, from insouciant driver to understated owner to trusted media *eminence gris.*

He was the consummate insider, the consummate gentleman and among the very last of the privateer breed.

With F1 teams now costing hundreds of millions of dollars per season instead of merely a few million, private entrant Rob Walker, shown here at The Glen in 1972, was a vanishing species even back then.

Rob Walker with his stopwatch at the ready focuses up-track during Friday's practice at The Glen, 1972.

FRANK WILLIAMS, CBE
England April 16, 1942

Frank loves racing, competing, winning, succeeding. And for years, he perched at the top of the motor racing universe, winning nine Constructors championships over 17 years. His Williams car and Williams team and Williams name were proven the best in the world.

He started out hard-scrabble. But he had energy and ambition and an irresistible personality. From tiny tot on, he was iron filings drawn to the magnet of motor racing. As a kid, he hitched to races all over England. Later he drove elderly racers in whatever events he could get to. By his twenties he was also running a spare parts business out of a flat he shared with his pal Piers Courage. Whenever his phone service was disconnected for lack of payment, he would hop down the street to a public phone box to do business.

Opening Frank Williams Racing Cars in the mid-1960s, he became an official Brabham dealer. This presented him with the chance to race an F3 Cooper, but he soon realized that he'd never reach the heights he sought as a driver. That was a problem he solved quickly and typically: He bought a Brabham F3, hired Piers to race it, and became a team owner. Frank Owen Garbett Williams was all in.

Three years later, he was able to buy a year-old F1 Brabham for Piers to run in the big league. Courage promptly took a 2nd to Graham Hill at Monaco, two 5^{ths} at Silverstone and Monza and a 2nd to Jochen Rindt at Watkins Glen. Piers finished the 1969 season with 16 championship points (a win back then was worth nine points), putting him 8th in the driver standings.

Frank's open personality, sparkling enthusiasm and sense of fun set the tone for the whole team. His wife, Ginny, was ever-present and ever ready with snacks and smiles and support both "fuzzy" and financial.

It all came crashing down on June 21, 1970. At the Dutch Grand

Prix, Piers was killed in a grisly crash. The heavy personal and team loss unmoored the Williams operation; Frank had lost not only his long-time friend but his dreams for the future. He tried to carry on, but he ended up foundering for the next few years. Eventually, his lifelong character traits of grit, bouyancy, resolve, recovery, persistence and dynamism finally righted his ship. In 1976, he sold that team and started all over a second time with his new Williams Grand Prix Engineering. By 1980, Alan Jones drove Williams to its first World Constructors Championship.

Over the next 17 years, Frank brought aboard Patrick Head and Adrian Newey; BMW, Renault, Honda and Mercedes; Nigel Mansell, Damon Hill, Alain Prost and Jacques Villeneuve. At various times, they and many others all fit into the famous Williams family that one driver described as "warm and cuddly", due mainly to Virginia's ministrations. The focus of Frank himself was and still is on *winning*, and he doesn't mind who does it, just so a Williams car crosses the finish line first.

March 8, 1986. Frank had just finished some pre-season testing in France and was headed for the airport and home when the car he was driving went off the road and flipped onto its roof. The crash left Frank paralyzed from the neck down. Permanently.

Again, his personal resolve surged to the surface, and just four months later, he attended practice for the British GP. His wheelchair became the vehicle that would then roll him to every single race in 1987 and beyond as he started over a third time.

A strong common thread running through any tales about the Williams team and about Frank is *integrity*. To hear some non-Williams people tell it, the Williams honesty is a lone beacon in the dense fog that is Formula One. Such a viewpoint, of course, makes every other team a slimy toad. Sure, where hundreds of millions are at stake, the hunt for an edge is ruthless and never-ending. And yes, extreme competitiveness can cloud judgment. And true, on rare occasions there's eavesdropping, spying, bribery, espionage, etc. But I believe most teams want to avoid the abyss of ethical transgressions, if for no other reason than if they try it, there are plenty of watchdogs around (such as other teams) to start howling.

At Williams, amidst all the hard work and glory and tragedies and success lurked the seeds of trouble. In racing as in life, it's not so much an action but the *reaction* that determines outcomes. A triple whammy hit Williams in the late 1990s. In 1996 Adrian Newey left the team (and it can't be coincidence that 1997 saw the last and most recent Constructors title for Williams). The next year, engine-supplier Renault pulled out. And in 1998, a new contract—the Concorde Agreement—was signed with Bernie Ecclestone's F1 management group that appeared to be to no one's benefit but Bernie and Ferrari. (The Concorde Agreement dictated the apportionment among the teams and Bernie's companies of revenue from TV rights, sponsor millions, ticket sales, entry fees, etc., amounting by the 2000s to well over half a *billion* dollars per year. With new owners Liberty Media, stay tuned.)

Toil and trouble only begot more toil and trouble. By the turn of the Millenium, Williams cars were sinking in the yearly constructor rankings, and no Williams drivers got within sniffing distance of the world title.

So much for the actions. What of Williams' reactions?

The energy and dreams of Frank Williams were still afloat. He'd already started over three times, and if he had to do it a fourth time, he would. And he did. In 2004 he brought in a slew of new people, including a new technical director.

But nothing changed. Got worse, if anything.

In 2006 he made more wholesale changes in personnel, but they swam against a tide of losing both major sponsorship money and free engines. Williams hung well beneath the surface, bobbing around down in 8th and 9th place among the ten or eleven teams. Gone was the private helicopter and the private plane, victims of a tightening budget; therefore, gone, too, was Frank's means of getting to and from races with any degree of ease.

In 2011, more tsunamis pounded in with the resignation of the technical director, chief aerodynamicist, chief operations engineer, and others including Frank's designer/colleague/part team owner Patrick Head. Not enough problems? This was also the year that the Williams operations floated an IPO on the Frankfurt stock exchange, meaning that Frank now would have stockholders who would demand profitability. In early 2012, the Williams chairman Adam Parr resigned. In early 2013, Ginny passed away. Hardly comparable but a blow nonetheless, at the end of 2013, driver Pastor Maldonado departed, taking his bag of $30M sponsorship money with him.

Watching all this, one is astonished at the continual and profound changes in personnel, engines, formulae, health, sponsorship, finances, etc. over the last decades. How often can an outfit survive such major upheavals? How often can essential leadership come and go without fatal damage? Could Frank re-invent the operation a *seventh* time?

He not only could—he *did*. In 2011, the Williams team finished 9th of the 11 teams in the Constructors championship. In 2012, 8th. In 2013, 9th. In 2014 and 2015, a strong stable of drivers, the strong Mercedes engines and a strong crew pulled the team into 3rd behind the runaway winner Mercedes factory (Red Bull took 2nd). But Williams slipped to 5th at the end of 2016 and 2017, and in 2018 it sank right to the bottom despite Frank and his daughter/board member/deputy team principal Claire giving it all they've got. That's the Williams way—but they haven't had a victory since 2012, and that one came after a seven-year drought.

Whatever happens in the future, as one looks back, the Williams marque carves a trail of glory across the decades and joins the pantheon of the greatest teams in motor racing.

Often unbeatable in the 1980s and 1990s, the Williams marque reflected the grit of its founder, Frank Williams, right, shown chatting with noted photographer David Phipps at the Questor GP.

APPENDIX

The World Champion Drivers and Constructors

Points are earned by *all* drivers on the constructor's team and are cumulative; that is why the Constructors title and the World Driving title sometimes go to two different teams (the very first year, for example). Unless noted under "Driver's Marque" both titles went to the same team. The award for constructors started in 1958.

Year	Constructors Title	Driving Title	Driver's Marque
1950		Nino Farina	Alfa Romeo
1951		Juan Manuel Fangio	Alfa Romeo
1952		Alberto Ascari	Ferrari
1953		Alberto Ascari	Ferrari
1954		Juan Manuel Fangio	Mercedes Benz
1955		Juan Manuel Fangio	Mercedes Benz
1956		Juan Manuel Fangio	Ferrari
1957		Juan Manuel Fangio	Maserati
1958	Vanwall	Mike Hawthorn	Ferrari
1959	Cooper	Jack Brabham	
1960	Cooper	Jack Brabham	
1961	Ferrari	Phil Hill	
1962	BRM	Graham Hill	
1963	Lotus	Jim Clark	
1964	Ferrari	John Surtees	
1965	Lotus	Jim Clark	
1966	Brabham	Jack Brabham	
1967	Brabham	Denny Hulme	
1968	Lotus	Graham Hill	
1969	Matra	Jackie Stewart	
1970	Lotus	Jochen Rindt (posthumous)	
1971	Tyrrell	Jackie Stewart	
1972	Lotus	Emerson Fittipaldi	
1973	Lotus	Jackie Stewart	Tyrrell
1974	McLaren	Emerson Fittipaldi	

Year	Constructors Title	Driving Title	Driver's Marque
1975	Ferrari	Niki Lauda	
1976	Ferrari	James Hunt	McLaren
1977	Ferrari	Niki Lauda	
1978	Lotus	Mario Andretti	
1979	Ferrari	Jody Scheckter	
1980	Williams	Alan Jones	
1981	Williams	Nelson Piquet	Brabham
1982	Ferrari	Keke Rosberg	Williams
1983	Ferrari	Nelson Piquet	Brabham
1984	McLaren	Niki Lauda	
1985	McLaren	Alain Prost	
1986	Williams	Alain Prost	McLaren
1987	Williams	Nelson Piquet	
1988	McLaren	Ayrton Senna	
1989	McLaren	Alain Prost	
1990	McLaren	Ayrton Senna	
1991	McLaren	Ayrton Senna	
1992	Williams	Nigel Mansell	
1993	Williams	Alain Prost	
1994	Williams	Michael Schumacher	Benetton
1995	Benetton	Michael Schumacher	
1996	Williams	Damon Hill	
1997	Williams	Jacques Villeneuve	
1998	McLaren	Mika Häkkinen	
1999	Ferrari	Mika Häkkinen	McLaren

Year	Constructors Title	Driving Title	Driver's Marque
2000	Ferrari	Michael Schumacher	
2001	Ferrari	Michael Schumacher	
2002	Ferrari	Michael Schumacher	
2003	Ferrari	Michael Schumacher	
2004	Ferrari	Michael Schumacher	
2005	Renault	Fernando Alonso	
2006	Renault	Fernando Alonso	
2007	Ferrari	Kimi Räikkönen	
2008	Ferrari	Lewis Hamilton	McLaren
2009	Brawn	Jenson Button	
2010	Red Bull	Sebastian Vettel	
2011	Red Bull	Sebastian Vettel	
2012	Red Bull	Sebastian Vettel	
2013	Red Bull	Sebastian Vettel	
2014	Mercedes Benz	Lewis Hamilton	
2015	Mercedes Benz	Lewis Hamilton	
2016	Mercedes Benz	Nico Rosberg	
2017	Mercedes Benz	Lewis Hamilton	
2018	Mercedes Benz	Lewis Hamilton	

Index

Entries in **boldface** indicate the biography.
P indicates a photo page and/or caption.
Only *significant* mentions are listed here for championships, circuits, marques and teams, or this Index would run a zillion pages.

Lightning Source UK Ltd.
Milton Keynes UK
UKHW022240130522
402993UK00009B/313/J